Write On

A Guide for Practice and Progression
in English Writing

A guide for practice
and progression in English writing

WRITE ON

Sungkyun Language Institute

Sungkyunkwan University Press

Contents

Building Blocks

Research Skills

Preface

Dear Students,

Writing in another language can be a daunting task as even native speakers who have a natural talent for writing need to practice and develop their craft in their own language. However, just because writing is a difficult skill to master, does not mean it is an impossible task.

The motto for this book is, "A textbook for practice and progression." Therefore, not only do we provide innumerous exercises ranging from basic to difficult to help students understand and practice essential grammar rules and structural guidelines, but we have also included "signposts." We hope that these "signposts" will continually reinforce basic concepts while students are applying their knowledge in writing and help students see connections between different skills. We have also created a section showing the relationship between paragraph and essay writing which we hope will make the transition from the one type of writing to the other more logical and thus more manageable.

In addition to grammar and structure practice, we prioritize research skills and anti-plagiarism methods in this book. While students usually understand that copying information from another person or source is wrong, they do not always know what techniques they can use to avoid plagiarism. Therefore, this book also has a section devoted to paraphrasing, summarizing, citations, and researching skills. We believe this part is not only helpful for developing English skills but can also be applied to academic writing in all fields of study.

Finally, we hope this book will give students the information and practice necessary to develop their English ability and give them more confidence in their general ability to organize and develop their writing. We believe that this book will create a valuable foundation from which students can produce solid academic work in all subjects.

Cameron Bramall
Bridget McGregor
David Roberts

Acknowledgements

The authors wish to thank Irene Park, Praise Lee, Richard Murray, and Malcolm Wray for their thoughtful guidance and steadfast support throughout the writing process. Without them this process would never have come to fruition.

The Writing Process

This section helps students develop and master the three basic writing structures: sentences, paragraphs, and essays. The first part of this section covers different kinds of sentence structure to ensure students use a variety sentence types in their writing. The next part explores paragraphs by teaching students how to brainstorm, develop parts of the paragraph, and maintain consistency throughout the entire piece of writing. After students have learned about paragraphs, they will learn how to transition into writing essays, including brainstorming, developing introductory paragraphs, structuring body paragraphs, creating supporting evidence or arguments, and making effective concluding paragraphs. Once students finish this section, they should feel more confident in their ability to write well-structured, well-developed, and well-argued paragraphs and essays in English.

This section covers:

- Format
- Pre-Writing
- Sentences
- Paragraphs
- Essays

1 Format

Unless you are specifically told otherwise, you are expected to type and print writing assignments. It is important that the assignment is arranged and presented in an appropriate way, and this is called "format." The format that is presented here is called Modern Language Association style (MLA). Other styles are available.

Activity 1

The following paragraphs are about the history of Sungkyunkwan University. The content is the same, but the format is different. Read the two paragraphs and pay attention to the format. Identify the errors in the first that are corrected in the second.

Sungkyunkwan University (SKKU) was founded in 1398 as a Confucius school of learning for the privileged and upper class.
The original campus is located in what is now Myeongnyun Dong, Seoul. During the Japanese occupation from 1911, the school was renamed Kyonghagwon, and remained so until 1946 when the occupation ended and the original name, Sungkyunkwan, was restored. Over the next three decades, SKKU grew in size and reputation.
Facing an increasing student enrollment, and restricted by limited space around the campus in central Seoul, SKKU expanded its campus in 1978 and developed a second site in suwon that would house the school of natural sciences.
Currently, the suwon campus has an enrollment of around 15,000 students, up from 5000 when it opened.
Together the two campuses provide the largest center of learning in South Korea, with the greatest student population.

Sungkyunkwan University

Sungkyunkwan University (SKKU) was founded in 1398 as a Confucius school of learning for the privileged and upper class. The original campus is located in what is now Myeongnyun-dong, Seoul. During the Japanese occupation from 1911, the school was renamed Kyonghagwon, and remained so until 1946 when the occupation ended and the original name, Sungkyunkwan, was restored. Over the next three decades, SKKU grew in size and reputation. Facing an increasing student enrollment and restricted by limited space around the campus in central Seoul, SKKU expanded its campus in 1978 and developed a second site in Suwon that now houses the school of natural sciences. Currently, the Suwon campus has an enrollment of around 15,000 students, up from 5,000 when it opened. Together the two campuses provide the largest center of learning in South Korea, with the greatest student population.

Format Guideline

Check

	Check
Line space Set the line space to 2.0.	☐
Title All writing assignments require a title centered at the top of the first page. The title should not be a sentence, and it should follow all of the capitalization, font, and size guidelines.	☐
Indent Indent the first line of the paragraph five spaces, or adjust the indent settings and hit the TAB key.	☐
Size Use font size 12.	☐
Font Use a plain font such as Times New Roman. Do not use a fancy font.	☐
Margins Leave a margin on each side of the page. Do not write in the margins.	☐
Check Check your paper for spelling and grammar. Do not make handwritten corrections.	☐
Personal details Put your full name, class, and student number in the top corner of the first page.	☐

2 Pre-Writing

The aim of pre-writing is to focus thoughts, develop ideas, and explore your topic in preparation for writing. There are a number of methods that can be used in pre-writing.

Free Writing

The aim is to write continuously on the page without stopping to think. Write whatever comes to mind, and do not worry about grammar, spelling, or word choice. It can be done on the computer or on paper. You might start with a general topic (for example, jobs) or a theme (for example, descriptive writing), but you can also write completely freely and see what develops.

The keys to effective free writing:

- Set a time limit
- Write for the whole of the allotted time
- Write down everything that comes into your head, regardless of logic or quality

Activity 1

Practice free writing for ten minutes, and then read your work. Were the ideas connected, or did they jump around from topic to topic? Read your partner's work.

List

Listing is a form of brainstorming in which writers list of all the ideas that come to their mind in a set time.

Seoul

Blue House	Hongdae	Crowded
Cheonggyecheon	Museums	Big
Universities	City Hall	Pollution
Subway	Palaces	Exciting
Capital city	Bus	Han River

Activity 2

In your notebook, list ideas for one of the following topics.

University | Friend | Sport | Hero

Mind Map

A mind map is a great way to organize ideas according to relationships or common features.

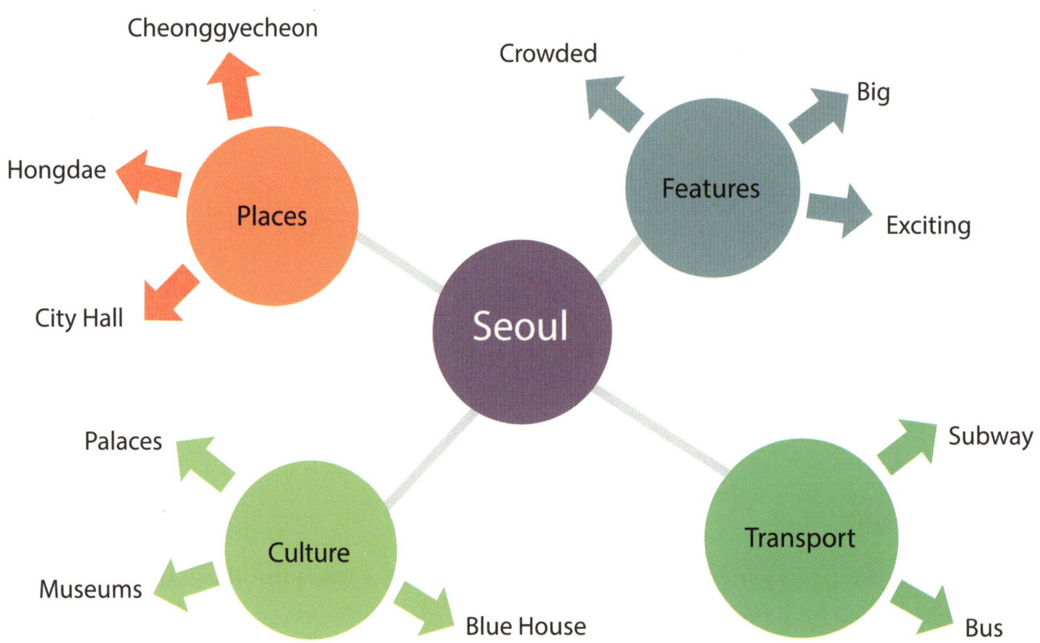

Activity 3

Make a mind map to connect your ideas from Activity 2.

Web Search

These days, the first place people go for ideas is often the Internet. The Internet gives us access to an almost unlimited amount of information, all at our fingertips. While the Internet should not be the only resource, it is a valuable tool.

Activity 4

Use the Internet to research one of the following topics. Use at least three sources.

Christmas	Chuseok	Easter	Halloween

Cut and paste the information relevant to the topic into a Word document. Copy the URL for each source onto the document. Each source and its content should be color coded or in a different font. Arrange the information in a logical way so it flows as a single piece. Add a title and list the URLs at the end of the document.

Journal

Many writers keep a journal of thoughts, ideas, and questions. This can be a creative tool for developing ideas for future writing projects.

Activity 5

The methods described in this chapter can be used individually or they can be used together as a longer process. Practice prewriting by following this process.

1. Free write for ten minutes.
2. Take one idea from the free writing section as a topic, and make a list of related ideas.
3. Organize these ideas into a clear, logical mind map.
4. Do a web search on the topic being developed, and gather three good sources.
5. Arrange your ideas and the information from the web search into a logical order.

3 Sentences

A sentence is a complete idea, and it contains a subject and a verb. In other words, a sentence is composed of one or more clauses, which are grammatical units containing at least an explicit or implied subject, and a predicate. Clauses may be independent (IC) or dependent (DC).

What is an independent clause?

An independent clause is the part of a sentence that can stand by itself because it includes a subject, verb, and complete idea.

What is a dependent clause?

A dependent clause requires an independent clause to make a complete sentence because it is incomplete by itself.

Types of Sentences

Type of Sentence	Sentence Construction
Simple Sentence	One IC
Compound Sentence	More than one IC, no DC
Complex Sentence	One IC, at least one DC
Compound-Complex Sentence	More than one IC, one or more DC

Grammar Tip Complete Sentences

- Start with a capital letter
- Finish with a period (.), a question mark (?), or an exclamation mark (!)
- Contain at least one independent clause (IC), which includes a subject (S), a verb (V), and a complete idea

Capital letter S V V Period

A sneaky burglar broke into my house and ate all my spaghetti.

IC

Capital letter S V

London's famous underground "tube" system is in trouble because the ancient infrastructure was not designed to cope with the demands of modern society.

Period

Sentence Structure and Variety

Because writers do not want to repeatedly use the same type of sentence structure in their writing, they use different types of sentences to make their writing more effective. This section will help students identify and construct different sentence types.

Simple Sentences and Sentence Fragments

The simple sentence is a single clause that includes a subject, verb, and a complete idea. Simple sentences are also known as independent clauses when they are part of longer sentences. Sentences that are incomplete are called sentence fragments.

Examples:
Simple Sentence: The animal was sick.
Sentence Fragment: Because the animal was sick.

Activity 1

Read the following sentences, and identify the subject and verb in each section. If the sentence is a sentence fragment, finish the sentence yourself.

1. The monkeys were hungry.
2. The massive storm destroyed many of the trees in the jungle.
3. While walking in the jungle.
4. Who gave a lecture on gorillas?
5. Who gave a lecture on gorillas.
6. Because the zoo was closed.
7. The biologist gave the school children a tour of the zoo.
8. The biologist who studies monkeys.
9. The conservation program focuses on preserving natural habitat.
10. After the lecture on preserving natural habitat.

Compound Sentences

Compound sentences are two simple sentences joined by a comma with a coordinating conjunction (FANBOYS). Each coordinating conjunction shows a relationship.

Coordinating Conjunctions	Example
For (cause)	He was late for class, **for** he missed the bus.
And (addition)	He is rich, **and** she likes shopping.
Nor (negative choice)	She did not want help, **nor** did she ask for it.
But (contrast)	He wanted to meet his friends, **but** he had to study.
Or (positive choice)	We can go to Caribbean Bay, **or** we can go to Everland.
Yet (contrast/concession)	He is a heavy smoker, **yet** he is a good athlete.
So (effect)	It rained last weekend, **so** the picnic was cancelled.

Punctuation Tip — Commas in Compound Sentences

When joining two independent clauses with a conjunction, a comma (,) is used after the first clause and before the conjunction.

Two simple sentences: Rabbits are plant eaters. Tigers eat meat.
One compound sentence: Rabbits are plant eaters, **but** tigers eat meat.

If the sentence contains only one independent clause and a conjunction, a comma is not used because it is not a compound sentence.

Compound sentence: Rabbits eat grass, **and** rabbits eat weeds.
Simple sentence: Rabbits eat grass and weeds.

Activity 2

Write a "C" (compound) or "NC" (not compound) beside the following sentences.

1. Elephants eat leaves and fruit.
2. Elephants eat leaves, fruit, and grass.
3. Elephants eat leaves, fruit, and grass, but they never eat fish.
4. Bats eat so many different kinds of food.
5. Bears sleep most of the winter, so they are hibernating animals.
6. Bats are active at night, for they are nocturnal animals.
7. Camels have one or two humps on their backs.
8. Neither cats nor dogs live in water.
9. Pandas' bodies are suited for eating meat, yet they eat bamboo.
10. Dolphins cannot live on land, nor can whales live on land.

Complex Sentences

Complex sentences are independent clauses joined by subordinating conjunctions to subordinating (or dependent) clauses. In complex sentences, commas are only used if the dependent clause comes first.

Because their tusks are ivory, elephants are sometimes killed by poachers.
Elephants are sometimes killed by poachers **because** their tusks are ivory.

Subordinating Conjunctions

The following table shows the subordinating conjunctions using "ON A WHITE BUS."

Subordinating Words	Example
Only if	I will cook **only if** you wash the dishes.
Now that	**Now that** I feel better, I can go back to work.
After, although, as	**Although** the fish smelled bad, it tasted good.
When, whenever, where, wherever, while, whereas, whether or not	Julia wore glasses **when** she was young.
If, in case	**If** you leave the room, please lock the door.
Though	**Though** she was angry, she smiled.
Even though, even if	**Even** if you are on a diet, you need to eat.
Because, before	**Before** she became a vegetarian, she loved beef.
Unless, until	**Unless** they hurry up, they will be late.
Since, so that	**Since** he was young, he has loved dogs.

Activity 3

Insert an appropriate subordinating conjunction in the following sentences. In addition, identify the independent and dependent clauses.

1. ____________________ rats carry diseases, people do not want them in homes.
2. ____________________ baby birds can fly, their parents bring them food.
3. ____________________ kangaroos are babies, they live in their mother's pouch.
4. ____________________ many snakes are harmless, many people are afraid of them.
5. Baby frogs can live on land ____________________ they grow legs and lungs.
6. Sharks do not attack humans ____________________ they are hungry.
7. ____________________ skunks feel in danger, they expel a horrible spray.
8. Kittens cannot open their eyes ____________________ they are born.

Activity 4

Interview your partner. Take notes of your partner's information in your notebook, and use them to write a mix of compound and complex sentences underneath your notes. Use the following questions as a starting point, but make sure you think of some interesting questions of your own.

1. What musical instrument would you like to learn?
2. Which film star would you like to play you in the movie of your life?
3. What do you look for in a boyfriend or girlfriend?
4. What animal best represents you?
5. Which species of animal would you exterminate?
6. Which household chore is your least favorite?
7. Which country would you never want to visit?
8. Which celebrity would you like to meet?

Punctuation Tip: Joining Independent Clauses with Semicolons

A semicolon (;) can be used to join two independent clauses. It is placed after the first independent clause, followed by a transition word and a comma. The word following the semicolon is not capitalized. This is another way to add variety to your writing.

IC + semicolon (;) + transition word + comma (,) + IC

Example: Mosquitoes are usually harmless; **however**, they sometimes carry diseases like malaria.

Some sentences can even be joined without a transition word if the ideas in both clauses are closely related.

Example: Mosquitoes can carry malaria; they can also carry dengue fever.

Semicolon Practice

Correct the following sentences by using semicolons.

Example: Mosquitoes carry diseases like malaria; they also transmit dengue fever.

Activity 5

Based on the previous punctuation tip, use semicolons to connect the following sentences.

1. Alligators have sharp teeth. They do not make good pets.

____

2. Cows are raised for their meat. They are also raised for milk.

____

3. Chickens have wings. They are not able to fly for long periods.

____

4. Camels store water in their humps. They can walk long distances without water.

____

Activity 6

Coordinating conjunctions, subordinating conjunctions, and transition word often convey similar relationships. Using the words given, complete the table.

Coordinating conjunctions: for, and, but, yet, so.

Subordinating conjunctions: while, so that, even though, though, since, due to, because, although

Transitions: nevertheless, because of this, on the other hand, therefore, thus.

Relationship	Words
Addition	
Contrast	
Effect	
Cause	

Activity 7

Rewrite the following sentences in another type of sentence. For instance, try changing a compound sentence into a complex sentence.

Example: Mosquitoes are usually harmless; **however**, they sometimes carry diseases. (;)
Mosquitoes are usually harmless, but they sometimes carry diseases. (compound)
Although mosquitoes are usually harmless, they sometimes carry diseases. (complex)

1. Elephants eat leaves, fruit, and grass, but they never eat fish.

____

2. Because some rats carry diseases, people do not want them in homes.

____

3. Bears sleep most of the winter, so they are hibernating animals.

____

4. Pandas' bodies are suited for eating meat, yet they eat bamboo.

____

5. Although many snakes are harmless, many people are still afraid of them.

____

6. Elephants eat leaves and fruit, and they also eat grass.

____

Compound-complex Sentences

This sentence type combines compound and complex sentences, and/or semicolons into the same sentence. The following simple sentences can be combined into one compound–complex sentence.

Original Passage:
The American Kennel Club recognizes over one hundred and fifty dog breeds. Border Collies are one of the most intelligent breeds. Afghan Hounds are considered one of the least intelligent.

Compound-complex Sentence:
The American Kennel Club recognizes over one hundred and fifty dog breeds, **and** Border Collies are one of the most intelligent dog breeds **while** Afghan Hounds are considered one of the least intelligent.

Activity 8

Use the skills practiced so far to combine the following sentences. Remember to use a variety of sentence types.

1. Pigs are often considered dirty. Pigs do not sweat very much. Pigs cover themselves in mud on hot days to keep cool.

____

____

2. Rabbits can have four to twelve babies in each pregnancy. Rabbits are pregnant for thirty days. One rabbit can have eight hundred descendants in nine months.

____

____

3. Chameleons have many talents. Chameleons can sleep upside down. Chameleons can change color in reaction to temperature changes. Chameleons' eyes can turn independently of one another.

____

____

4. Chimpanzees use tools like sticks to find food. Chimpanzees are very similar to humans. The two species share 98.4% of the same genetic material. Chimpanzees can recognize themselves in a mirror.

____

____

5. Many oysters change their sex several times in their lives. Shrimp are born male. Shrimp become female as they get older. Some animals do not have a stable sex.

____

____

Comma Splices

Comma splices are incomplete sentences that incorrectly combine independent clauses with a comma.

Example:
Horses can sleep standing up, they can also sleep lying down.

There are four ways to correct comma splices:

1. Use a period after the first independent clause to create two separate sentences.
   Horses can sleep standing up. They can also sleep lying down.

2. Insert a semicolon after the first independent clause to create a compound sentence.
   Horses can sleep standing up; they can also sleep lying down.

3. Insert a coordinating conjunction after the comma to create a compound sentence.
   Horses can sleep standing up, and they can also sleep lying down.

4. Insert a subordinating conjunction at the beginning of the clause to create a complex sentence.
   While horses can sleep standing up, they can also sleep lying down.

Activity 9

Correct the following comma splices.

1. Chickens eat seeds, they also eat small animals like lizards or mice.

   ____

2. Sheep are raised for their wool, they are also raised for their milk and meat.

   ____

3. Many parrots can learn to speak human languages, they are popular as pets.

   ____

4. In some areas, tigers are nearly extinct, they are hunted for their beautiful fur.

   ____

5. Turtles appeared about 215 million years ago, they are one of the oldest orders of reptiles.

   ____

4 Paragraphs

A paragraph is an organizational unit or chunk in writing that comprises a group of sentences on a single theme or topic. Most writing is organized into themed chunks ranging in length from a single sentence to a dozen or more sentences. Regardless of the length, these chunks should develop the main idea in a clear and logical way.

A paragraph may stand by itself or be one part of a longer piece of work. In academic writing, paragraphs are often used to answer short questions, give definitions or descriptions, or give opinions. If you can write good paragraphs, you can write good essays. This unit starts with the essentials of paragraph writing and then moves on to how to combine and expand individual paragraphs to build essays.

Paragraph Structure

A good paragraph usually has three basic parts, as shown in the basic outline below.

Title

1. Topic sentence

2. Supporting sentences
- **a**. Supporting detail
- **b**. Supporting detail
- **c**. Supporting detail

3. Concluding sentence

Title: Africa's Most Dangerous Animal

1. Topic sentence

Africa's most dangerous animal is the hippopotamus.

2. Supporting sentences

a. Physical characteristics powerful animal, three meters in length, weighs over three tones, can outrun a human, has powerful jaws that can easily bite a person in half.

b. Temperament - very bad tempered, anyone who gets in between an adult hippopotamus and its calf or the water is likely to be attacked.

c. Statistics – Kills more than 500 people each year, more than any other large African animal.

3. Concluding sentence

The power, temperament, and number of victims of the hippopotamus make it the most feared animal in Africa.

When put together, the pieces create a strong outline for a logical and coherent paragraph.

Africa's Most Dangerous Animal

Africa's most dangerous animal is the hippopotamus. First of all, it is a very powerful animal. It grows up to three meters in length, weighs over three tones, and can outrun a human. It also has extremely powerful jaws that can easily bite a person in half. Secondly, the hippopotamus is very bad tempered. Anyone who gets in between an adult hippopotamus and its calf or the water is likely to be attacked. Finally, the hippopotamus is responsible for more than 500 deaths each year, which is more than any other large African animal. In conclusion, the power, temperament, and number of victims of the hippopotamus make it the most feared animal in Africa.

The Topic Sentence

What is a topic sentence? The topic sentence can be seen as the key to your paragraph. It is the most important part of the paragraph, and it opens the door to your opinions or ideas about the topic. It gives the reader the main idea and must clearly state what the paragraph is about. As it is usually the first sentence, it must also catch the reader's attention.

A topic sentence should do the following:

Get the attention of the reader
This is your opportunity to draw your reader into your paragraph.

Introduce the main point of the paragraph
The topic sentence should prepare the reader for what information you are going to give them.

Contain a topic and a controlling idea
The topic sentence should state the theme of the paragraph and the more specific focus within the theme.

Plant a question
The topic sentence should leave a question in the mind of the reader, and this is what will be explored in the paragraph.

A topic sentence has a topic and controlling idea. The topic is the thing being written about, and the controlling idea is the angle or point of focus.

Topic + Controlling idea = Topic sentence

Topic — Controlling idea

Example 1: Apoptosis, or programmed cell death, **has three qualities that make it a potential treatment for cancer.**

Example 2: Despite their similar appearance, there are **several important differences** between **tomato sauce and red pepper paste.**

Controlling idea — Topics

Activity 1

Read the following topic sentences, put the topic in parentheses, and underline the controlling idea.

Example: (Brunel) <u>revolutionized civil engineering through three landmark projects.</u>

1) There are several advantages of learning to cook.

2) In the winter, people can avoid injuries by taking certain precautions.

3) My fear of dogs began when I was a child.

4) There are several disadvantages to online shopping.

5) My holiday to Hawaii was the best time of my life.

What makes a good topic sentence?

1. It is a complete sentence

Good example:
The old cat has one annoying habit.

Poor example: An incomplete sentence.
The old cat's one annoying habit.

2. It is a statement of belief

Good example:
The ugly cat should have won the cat show.

Poor example: A simple fact.
The ugly cat did not win the cat show.

3. It is iconic

Good example: Shows the direction the paragraph will take.
Their loyalty, affection, and intelligence make cats great pets.

Poor example: Does not show the direction.
Cats are great.

4. It has appropriate focus

Good example:
With her retractable claws, needle-sharp teeth, and lightning speed, the ugly old cat is a superior hunter.

Poor example 1: Too specific.
Slow-witted shrews foraging in my garden for tasty morsels as the sun sets on a warm summer evening should beware of the ugly old cat, who is a lethal hunter because of her cunning temperament, 20 millimeter claws that can pop in and out of her paws, and pointed teeth that fill her gaping mouth.

Poor example 2: Too broad.
The ugly cat is dangerous.

Activity 2

Look at the following topic sentences. For each one, state whether it is a good topic sentence or a poor one.

Example: It happened years ago when we lived on Stanford Road.
Poor topic sentence. No topic.

1. Horse racing is the sport of kings.

____

2. The moon is a round ball of rock that orbits Earth.

____

3. The man with the raincoat.

____

4. Hiking is one of the best types of exercise.

____

5. There are three steps in taking good photographs.

____

6. Why shouldn't I eat these poisonous berries?

____

7. My friend Ji Yeon is the best friend I have ever had.

____

8. Because you did!

____

9. Ostriches are birds.

____

10. Suzanne's success comes from the good decisions she made early on in her career.

____

Activity 3

Read the following paragraph and select the most appropriate topic sentence from the list below.

Peterborough

Topic sentence: ______________________________

First, Peterborough is known for Flagg Fen, which is an ancient Bronze Age settlement. The old town, which dates back to 1365 BCE, is one of the most important places in the country for studying ancient civilizations. The next historical site is Longthorpe, a picturesque village which features a Roman fort from the first century CE. The buildings in the village are all very old and traditional, yet they are all still lived in today. The third and most famous ancient structure is the Peterborough Cathedral. Its origins can be traced back to 655 CE, and it has been used as a place of worship since then. The imposing Early English Gothic West Front was built in the 12th century and, with its three huge arches, is unique in style and a very impressive sight. In conclusion, Peterborough's historic sites make it an interesting and important city.

a. Prince William lives in Peterborough, England.

b. The City of Peterborough, England, is known for several historic features.

c. It is a famous city with many old buildings.

d. Let me introduce my hometown, which is old, beautiful, and fantastic.

Activity 4

Create topic sentences for the topics below.

Smoking

____

Military service

____

Blood donation

____

The Introduction Sentence

The first sentence in a paragraph is usually the topic sentence. However, writers sometimes use the opening one or two (or more) sentences to provide background information. Like the topic sentence, the introduction sentence is usually more general than the supporting sentences. Unlike the topic sentence, the introduction sentence is not referred to in and supported by the supporting sentences. In most cases, the introduction sentence gives a general point to introduce the topic and then the topic sentence introduces the main idea which is not mentioned in the introduction sentence.

Activity 5

Read the paragraph below and identify the introduction sentence and the topic sentence.

Africa's Most Dangerous Animal

Africa is a large continent that is well known for its diverse and often dangerous wildlife. Surprisingly, the animal that is considered the most dangerous is the hippopotamus. First of all, the hippopotamus is a very powerful animal. It grows up to three meters in length, weighs over three tons, and can outrun a human. It also has extremely powerful jaws that can easily bite a person in half. Secondly, the hippopotamus is very bad tempered. Anyone who gets in between an adult hippopotamus and its calf or the water is likely to be attacked. Finally, the hippopotamus is responsible for more than 500 deaths each year, which is more than any other large African animal. In conclusion the power, temperament, and number of victims of the hippopotamus make it the most feared animal in Africa.

Activity 6

Write one or two introduction sentences to give background information that will introduce each of the following topic sentences.

Introduction sentence: ____________________

____

Topic sentence: Soccer is the greatest team sport in the world.

Introduction sentence: ____________________

____

Topic sentence: There are three key steps to a flawless complexion.

Supporting Sentences

In academic writing, it is necessary for the writer to provide support for their ideas. This might well require research and investigation on the part of the writer in order to gather sufficient support. The supporting information in a paragraph is given in the supporting sentences, the sentences that follow the topic sentence. They should always relate to the topic and back up the main idea.

Example: Topic sentence: My cat has three annoying habits.
1. Sleeping on me
2. Shedding fur
3. Leaving dead rodents under the refrigerator

Activity 1

Read the following paragraph and complete the exercises.

Fast Food Phobia

Fast food, particularly McDonald's, is an easy target for people who claim to care about health. However, there are good reasons to believe that McDonald's is not just a dietary evil. First of all, there is the assumption that McDonald's meals are fattening due to the high calorie content. In fact, according to a study by Queen's College in London, "A Big Mac contains just 510 calories, which is some way short of the recommended daily intake of 2,550 calories for men and 1,940 calories for women. Even the most calorific item on the menu, the Double Quarter Pounder with Cheese, only contains 740 calories" (17). The second common criticism leveled at McDonald's is the level of trans-fats. In reality, all meat contains trans-fats, so the same criticism must also be aimed at every restaurant with meat on their menu. McDonald's burgers contain about 1.5g per serving, which is just 8% of the daily limit recommended by the World Health Organization (23). Finally, the salt, or more specifically, sodium content of McDonald's meals is often attacked as a major health problem. The data shows this criticism is unjustified. The recommended daily intake of sodium for an adult is 1,500mg, and no more than 2,300mg. A Big Mac, McDonald's most famous and popular burger, contains just 1,040mg of sodium (12), which is well within the healthy limit. In summary, as with any other food, McDonald's can be part of a healthy diet as long as it is eaten in moderation.

1. Underline the topic sentence.

2. What are the three supporting ideas?

a) ______________________________

b) ______________________________

c) ______________________________

Activity 2

Add ideas to support each of the following topic sentences.

There are three important components to the perfect date.

1. ______________________________
2. ______________________________
3. ______________________________

There are several economic advantages to hosting the Olympic Games.

1. ______________________________
2. ______________________________
3. ______________________________

A monarchy serves important functions.

1. ______________________________
2. ______________________________
3. ______________________________

Evidence and Support

Each supporting sentence contains an idea that supports the topic sentence, along with supporting details or evidence to back up the idea. Supporting details are given in the form of examples, statistics, and quotations.

Examples

Examples are the easiest and most common supporting details. They are useful for adding interesting support to a paragraph and do not usually require as much research as quotes and statistics.

Example: Psychology graduates learn a range of skills that are desired by many employers, such as numerical and statistical skills, effective communication skills, and teamwork.

Statistics

Statistics are a good way of giving specific details using numbers. They can be very strong support for a point and can provide detailed and even surprising information.

Example: According to Professor Keeley at Newcastle University 28.7% of psychology graduates are attracted to accountancy, banking, and management, which are growth areas, compared with just 14% of IT graduates (Stubbs 2).

Quotations

Quotations are using the words of a respected authority on a subject to add support or credibility to your point. They are useful because they show the reader that your ideas are in line with those of experts in the field, and are therefore likely to be correct.

Example: According to Dr. Uffindel of the Bright Network, "It is true that these students know that if they want to apply their psychology theory in the workplace for a range of careers, they understand a period of further study and work experience-up to 12 months is necessary" (1).

Activity 3

Read the paragraph. Identify the relevant supporting sentences. What kind of support does the writer use? Underline any examples, statistics, and quotations.

The Most Employable Degree

A 2010 study showed that unemployment among recent graduates was at its highest since 1993 at 8.9% (BBC News). However, among the most successful were psychology graduates due to the skills learned, flexibility of the qualification, and practical experience gained on the course. Psychology graduates learn a range of skills that are desired by many employers, such as numerical and statistical skills, effective communication skills, and teamwork. Second, psychology graduates are often drawn to industries with more vacancies. According to Professor Keeley at Newcastle University, 28.7% of psychology graduates are attracted to accountancy, banking and management, which are growth areas, compared with just 14% of IT graduates (Stubbs 2). Finally, it is common for psychology students to gain practical experience in the workplace prior to graduation. According to Dr. Uffindell of the Bright Network, "It is true that these students know that if they want to apply their psychology theory in the workplace for a range of careers, they understand a period of further study and work experience–up to 12 months–is necessary" (1). Therefore, the skills, versatility, and experience gained by psychology graduates makes them comparatively successful in the job market.

Activity 4

Read the paragraph about McDonald's again and summarize the supporting details in the appropriate box.

Example:

Statistic:

Quotation:

Activity 5

Write a topic sentence on the following topics and give three supporting details.

Sport Fashion University

Topic sentence:

____

Supporting details:

____

____

____

____

Topic sentence:

____

Supporting details:

____

____

____

____

Topic sentence:

____

Supporting details:

____

____

____

____

Unity

It is important that all of the supporting sentences in a paragraph match the topic sentence. This means that they should relate to both the topic and the controlling idea. If you are writing a paragraph about the life of Joseph Merrick, then all the supporting sentences should relate directly to the life of Joseph Merrick. Furthermore, each supporting sentence should relate to a single aspect of his life. We should not have sentences that focus on the romantic relationships of Joseph Merrick's sister, or on the pets of Joseph Merrick.

There are two common problems relating to unity in paragraphs.
1. The paragraph contains sentences relating to more than one topic.
2. The paragraph contains sentences supporting more than one controlling idea.

Tip For a cohesive paragraph, repeat the key nouns throughout the paragraph. You can also use synonyms to keep the cohesion but add variety.

Activity 6

Read the paragraph below and identify the sentence that does not match the topic sentence. Does the paragraph contain a) more than one topic, or b) more than one controlling idea?

The Difficult Life of Joseph Merrick

Life in 1860s London was tough, but it was particularly difficult for "Elephant Man" Joseph Merrick. Merrick is one of a number of famous disabled people to have a film made about their extraordinary life, along with Cristy Brown (*My Left Foot*, 1989) and Rocky Dennis (*Mask*, 1985). Merrick was born with a severe growth problem meaning that bones on the right side of his body, including skull, ribs, arm, and leg, continued to grow throughout his life. This led to respiratory problems, speech impediments, and, most notably, a physically repulsive appearance. After being abandoned as a child, Merrick was picked up by a backstreet sideshow, where he was cruelly treated by the owner who made money from showing his unusual exhibit to a paying public. Merrick was treated as an animal, and it was assumed from his appearance that he was unintelligent. Eventually, he was rescued by Dr. Fredrick Treves, and they built a relationship together. Dr. Treves studied Merrick's condition but could not cure him. Merrick's condition continued to deteriorate and at the age of 27 he died in his sleep. In conclusion, Joseph Merrick's remarkable story reminds us that there is a person behind every face.

Activity 7

Read the paragraph, and identify the sentence that does not match the topic sentence. Does the paragraph contain a) two topics, or b) more than one controlling idea?

Ancient Seoul

Seoul, the capital of South Korea, has a number of historical sites. The most famous is Gyeongbok Palace, which was the residence of the monarchy until Emperor Yunghui (Sunjong) was dethroned during the Japanese occupation in 1910. Gyeongbok Palace was originally built in 1394 as one of the five great palaces of the Joseon Dynasty and is located in the center of the city. The second famous historical site in Seoul is Joggye Temple (Jogyesa), which has been a place of worship for over 600 years. It is located close to Gyeongbok Palace in the center of Seoul. Gyeongju, the capital of Shilla Dynasty, also contains many historical sites including the distinctive dome shaped tombs in which the remains of ancient rulers are buried. Another historical site in Seoul is the ancient fortress wall that was built to protect Hanyang, the capital of the Joseon Dynasty. The wall surrounds Seoul's four mountains, Naksan, Namsan, Bukansan, and Inwangsan and served to protect the city from invasions. In summary, these are just a few examples of the many historical sites in Seoul.

Connecting Words

Connecting words can be used to show the structure of a paragraph by indicating transitions from one supporting point to another. The table below shows some possible transition signal words and phrases.

Connecting Words and Phrases	
First, First of all, The first …, To begin with	The first idea in a series or sequence
Second, Secondly …	The second idea in a series or sequence
Third, Thirdly …	The third idea in a series or sequence
Next, Then, After that	The next idea in a series
In addition, Furthermore, Moreover	Making a further point
Similarly, Likewise	Comparing a similar idea
In contrast, On the other hand Nevertheless	Showing an opposing idea
Soon, Eventually	A transition over time in a time order paragraph

Activity 8

Read the paragraphs about ancient Seoul and Joseph Merrick once more and identify the connecting words and phrases.

Activity 9

Use the facts in the box below to create a series of supporting sentences on the topic below. Write a topic sentence to which all of your supporting sentences relate.

Ben Folds Five Facts

Career: Formed in 1993, broke up in 2000

Albums and chart success: *Ben Folds Five* (1995), did not chart in US Billboard 200

Whatever and Ever Amen (1997), reached no. 42 in US Billboard 200

The Unauthorized Biography of Reinhold Messner (1999), reached no. 35 in US Billboard 200

Members: Ben Folds (piano, vocals), Robert Sledge (bass guitar, vocals), Darren Jessee (drums, vocals)

From: North Carolina, USA

Most successful single: "Brick" (1997), reached no.19 in US Hot 100 Billboard Chart

Genre: Alternative rock

Known for: No guitar, songs that tell stories

Topic:

Title: ____________________

Topic sentence:

____

Supporting sentences: ____________________

____

____

____

____

____

____

Activity 10

Now do the same but with details from your own research.

Topic:

Title: ______________________________

Topic sentence:

____

____

____

____

Supporting sentences:

____

____

____

____

____

____

____

____

____

____

____

____

____

____

____

____

____

The Concluding Sentence

The concluding sentence is the final sentence in a paragraph. It finishes the paragraph in a satisfying way, and it helps the reader to cement their understanding of the ideas.

A concluding sentence should do the following:

Signal the end of the paragraph
Start your concluding sentence with a connecting word, such as Therefore, In conclusion, In summary.

Summarize the main points of the paragraph
What are the main points that support the topic or opinion?

Give a final comment about the topic
Sum up ideas as a single, concise comment that relates to the topic sentence.

Leave the reader thinking about the main ideas
Suggest a broader importance of ideas, such as consequences or possible future actions.

What makes a good concluding sentence?

Most paragraphs end with a concluding sentence. This sentence either reflects the topic sentence or reinforces the main points in the paragraph. Depending on the type of paragraph and the purpose of your writing, the topic sentence should do some or all of the following.

1. It is a complete sentence

Good example:
In conclusion, people love cats for their many endearing qualities.

Poor example: **This sentence has an unclear subject.**
In conclusion, there are many endearing qualities.

2. It indicates the end of the paragraph

Good example
In summary, people love cats for their many endearing qualities.

Poor example: **Does not clearly show the end of the paragraph.**
People love cats for their many endearing qualities.

3. It reinforces the main idea

Good example
Therefore, cats are great pets because of their devotion, cleverness, and friendliness.

Poor example: **Does not mention the main points.**
Cats are great pets.

4. It gives the reader a thinking point

Good example
Therefore, cats are the solution to Seoul's rat problem.

Poor example: **This states a simple fact.**
So, cats eat rats.

Tip

Do not put any new information in your concluding sentence.
Do not leave a personal message to the reader.

Conclusion Connecting Words

It is usually a good idea to start your concluding sentence with a clear signal that this is the end of your paragraph. This lets the reader know that there will be no new information and that the main point of the paragraph is about to be restated.

Examples

In conclusion	Therefore	We have seen that...
In summary	In brief	The evidence shows...
To sum up	While... is true, ...	It is clear that...
Thus	In short	From this, we can conclude that...

Activity 1

Read the following paragraph and use what you have learned so far to select the most appropriate concluding sentence from the options.

Ig Nobels

The Ig Nobels, an event that recognizes ingenuity in science research, is an awards ceremony like no other. The awards ceremony is organized by Annals of Improbable Research (AIR), which is a humor magazine presented as a parody of serious scientific literature. The self-stated aim of the Ig Nobels is "first make people laugh, and then make them think." Each year in October, scientists gather for the annual Ig Nobel awards ceremony, held at Harvard University, to see prizes distributed by genuine Nobel Prize winners. As with many awards ceremonies, the Ig Nobel prize winners are expected to make a speech, and the organizers have implemented an unusual but effective method for keeping these speeches from going on for too long. Miss Sweety Poo is a young girl who sits on the stage and as soon as she is tired of a speech repeats, "Please stop: I'm bored," until the speaker leaves the stage. While the ceremony is known for rewarding unusual research, there is often a use for the findings. For example, a study showing that malaria mosquitoes are attracted to the smell of human feet, and also, Limburger cheese has led to the development of effective mosquito traps. However, bad science is also recognized and rewarded as a criticism, such as with Jacques Benveniste. Benveniste's research "proved" that water has a memory, and that this information can be transmitted over the Internet.

____

____

a) While science is often seen as serious, the Ig Nobels give a more lighthearted angle focused on humor and entertainment.

b) In summary, the Ig Nobel awards are the biggest prizes in the science community.

c) In conclusion, the Ig Nobels are an unusual ceremony that began in 1991.

d) Furthermore, the unusual nature of the Ig Nobel awards makes them one of the highlights of the science calendar.

Types of Concluding Sentences

There are two main types of concluding sentences. The first is a summary of the main points of the paragraph while the second restates the topic sentence in different words.

Activity 2

Read the paragraph about the evolution of snakes.

1. Identify the topic sentence.
2. Identify the supporting details. How do they support the topic sentence?
   Then read the two example concluding sentences and identify which one is a summary of the main points of the paragraph and which is a restatement of the topic sentence.

Legless

Occasionally venomous, often depicted as cunning or deceitful, one thing that all snakes have in common is, besides their tail, an obvious absence of limbs. However, the evidence suggests that this has not always been the case. Experts believe that all lizards and snakes evolved from a reptilian common ancestor. Fossil evidence from the Cretaceous Period (144–65 million years ago) reveals at least four genera of early snakes; three in the Middle East and one in South America. The unusual feature of these snake fossils is the presence of short hind legs. These early snakes evolved from burrowing lizards with short and stubby limbs, and streamlined bodies. Over time, the front legs regressed until they were just short vestigial stumps. Fossils of primitive species, such as boas and pythons, still have these vestigial stumps as evidence of their legged ancestors. These are known as anal spurs and are used to grip during mating. Other modern snake species have lost even these traces of their lizard heritage. Genetic evidence reveals that evolution in Hox genes, which are responsible for limb development, resulted in the dramatic reduction on limb size and the eventual loss of functioning front and hind limbs in all modern snakes.

____

____

Concluding sentence 1: In conclusion, various lines of evidence show that primitive snakes had legs.

Concluding sentence 2: It is clear from fossil evidence, the anatomy of primitive modern snake species, and genetic analysis, that legless modern snakes evolved from legged ancestors.

Activity 3

There are four main steps in the process of writing a concluding sentence.

Step 1: Underline the topic sentence.

Step 2: Highlight the supporting ideas.

Step 3: Start the concluding sentence with a connecting word.

Step 4: Choose a type of concluding sentence.

Choosing a Pet

There are a number of things to consider when choosing a pet. Most importantly, people must carefully consider whether or not they are really ready to take on the responsibility of caring for an animal. Can they provide a pet with everything it will need in order to live a happy life in their care? Once someone is sure they can handle a pet, they must think about what they want from their pet. Fish look beautiful and are not too demanding in terms of time and space, but some consider them boring. Dogs and cats can be playful, affectionate, and can become great companions. Hamsters are popular and cute, but they are nocturnal. Some people want a more unusual pet, such as a lizard or an axolotl which need specialist equipment and knowledge. Finally, anyone thinking of buying a pet must consider what they are able to offer their animal. For someone with ample time and space, a dog might be a great option since they need exercise and attention. For someone who has never kept a pet before, it might be a good idea to start with a rabbit, which does not require training and does not live as long. It is irresponsible to get a pet which people cannot care for adequately.

Concluding sentence:

____

____

Activity 4

Read the following topic sentences from paragraphs elsewhere in the chapter, and rewrite them as concluding sentences.

Seoul, the capital of South Korea, has a number of historical sites.

Life in 1860s London was tough, but it was particularly difficult for "Elephant Man" Joseph Merrick.

Among the most successful were psychology graduates due to the skills learned, flexibility of the qualification, and practical experience gained on the course.

Despite the bad press, there are good reasons to reject the widely held belief that McDonald's is a dietary evil.

Paragraph Outlines

An outline is a useful stage of the planning process in any kind of academic or formal writing, including paragraphs, essays, and reports. It helps you to arrange your ideas in a logical way, and it makes the process of writing your final piece far simpler.

Topic: International Marriage

Topic sentence: In an increasingly globalized society, it is easier than ever before to meet people of other nationalities, and for the benefits to society, international couples, and their children, people should pursue intercultural romance and marriage.

Supporting detail 1: International marriage benefits the couple.

Supporting detail 2: International marriages will benefit society in the long term.

Supporting detail 3: International marriage benefits the children.

Concluding sentence: International relationships should be strongly encouraged.

Activity 1

Here are the components of an outline for a paragraph about yoga. Put them into a logical order by matching them with the relevant paragraph sections.

a. The Benefits of Yoga

b. Develops clear thinking, improves concentration.

c. Physical benefits.

d. Reduces fear, anger and worry, helps you to feel calm, develops self-confidence.

e. Mental benefits.

f. Improves blood circulation, improves digestion, makes you strong and flexible.

g. Emotional benefits.

h. Therefore, to build mental, physical and emotional health, consider practicing yoga.

i. Practicing yoga regularly can be good for your mind, your body and your emotions.

1. Topic ___a___
2. Topic sentence: ______
3. Supporting point 1: ______
4. Detail: ______
5. Supporting point 2: ______
6. Detail: ______
7. Supporting point 3: ______
8. Detail: ______
9. Concluding sentence: ______

Once the supporting points have been arranged in a logical order, you can begin to add details. At this point your paragraph really begins to take shape.

Topic: International Marriage

Topic sentence: In an increasingly globalized society, it is easier than ever before to meet people of other nationalities, and for the benefits to society, international couples, and their children, people should pursue intercultural romance and marriage.

Supporting detail 1: International marriage benefits the couple directly. The couple can learn each other's language and culture, as well as enjoy frequent travel opportunities.

Supporting detail 2: International marriages will benefit society in the long term. John Giddings, professor at Oxford University, suggests that intermarriage leads to greater genetic diversity, which could improve herd immunity in future generations (Giddings 41).

Supporting detail 3: International marriage benefits the children. Children of international parents have the advantage of identifying with two cultures, leading to more rounded opinions and richer life experience.

Concluding sentence: International relationships are nothing new and for the good of couples, society, and children, they are something that should be strongly encouraged.

Activity 2

Write three supporting points for each of the following topics.

Popular foreign food

1. ____________________
2. ____________________
3. ____________________

Technology of the future

1. ____________________
2. ____________________
3. ____________________

Travel experience

1. ____________________
2. ____________________
3. ____________________

Activity 3

Choose one of the topics from Activity 2 and develop it into a paragraph outline.

Topic: ____________________

____

Topic sentence: ____________________

____

a) Supporting detail 1:

____

____

____

b) Supporting detail 2:

____

____

____

c) Supporting detail 3:

____

____

____

Concluding sentence:

____

____

____

____

____

Activity 4

Write a paragraph about one of the topics below within 30 minutes. Start by brainstorming to gather and develop your ideas. Write an outline including a topic sentence, supporting details and a concluding sentence. Finally, write your paragraph.

Hometown	Disaster	Hobby

Plan your time: When writing within a time limit it is very important that you plan your time effectively. Here is a suggestion for planning your time for this writing task.

Brainstorm	-5 minutes
Outline	-7 minutes
Paragraph	-15 minutes
Check	-3 minutes

Paragraph checklist: Does your paragraph include the following:

Title	___
Format (see page 10)	___
Topic sentence	___
Relevant supporting details	___
Concluding sentence	___

Activity 5

Using what you have learned so far, write a paragraph on one of the topics below.

An interesting instrument	A common superstition
The perfect partner	A hero
A successful company	Technology of tomorrow

5 Essays

Essay Structure

There are three main parts to a five-paragraph essay. The first part is called the introduction, and it is a single paragraph. The second is the body. In a five-paragraph essay, the body is made up of three paragraphs. The final part of the essay is the conclusion, which like the introduction is a single paragraph. Look at the following chart to see how a paragraph and an essay are structured.

Paragraph	Essay
Topic sentence	**Introduction paragraph** • Hook • Background information • Thesis statement
A. Supporting detail	**Body paragraph 1** • Topic sentence • Supporting details • Concluding sentence
B. Supporting detail	**Body paragraph 2** • Topic sentence • Supporting details • Concluding sentence
C. Supporting detail	**Body paragraph 3** • Topic sentence • Supporting details • Concluding sentence
Concluding sentence	**Conclusion paragraph** • Restate overview • Summarize main points • Conclude memorably

Essay Example

Activity 1

Complete the following questions on "stress."

1. Life is full of stressful events (stressors). What causes you stress?

____

____

____

2. When you are stressed, how do you feel physically? What changes happen to you during times of stress? Check the physical symptoms that happen to you.

__ increased heart rate	__ hair loss	__ sweaty hands/palms
__ feeling irritable	__ muscle tension	__ shoulder or neck pain
__ headaches	__ dry mouth	__ butterflies in the stomach
__ skin irritations	__ insomnia	__ indigestion
__ shortness of breath	__ depression	__ feelings of anxiety

Responding to Stress

The term "stress" is often used to describe feelings of being overloaded and overwhelmed with the changes and demands of life. **Sheldon Cohen et al**, in their book *Measuring Stress*, describe stress **as the process in which "environmental demands tax or exceed the adaptive capacity of an organism, resulting in psychological and biological changes" (3).** These biological changes may be immediate and temporal, as well as, long term and constant and can have both positive and negative effects. *When examining the effects of stress on the body, it is common to discuss three biological responses: the hormonal response, the cardiovascular response, and the immune response.*

During times of emotional or physical stress, hormones are released into the circulatory system, resulting in a number of metabolic changes. **For example**, the release of hormones, such as epinephrine, norepinephrine, and dopamine are found to increase arousal and neural stimulation. When the body senses danger or a threat, the release of hormones by the adrenal medulla in the kidneys help to prepare a person to either fight or run away. The fight-or-flight response is a natural reaction to external threats or stress and has a number of beneficial effects, such as increasing muscular tension, and increasing alertness and awareness. While the fight-or-flight response can be advantageous in certain contexts, it can also inhibit performance in others. When concentration is needed, such as during exams or before giving a presentation, hormone release may actually reduce performance by suppressing short-term memory. *In terms of the effect of hormone release on the body, it is a significant factor influencing biological change.*

In addition to a hormonal response caused by stress, there is also a cardiovascular response triggered by neural and hormonal influences. Changes in heart rate, blood pressure and peripheral blood flow occur as a result of a release of hormones into the bloodstream and the activation of the autonomic nervous system. **Dr. David Engel, a cardiologist at Samsung Medical Center,** describes the cardiovascular response as "non-specific" meaning that different stressors or tasks affect the cardiovascular system and indeed people, in different ways **(77)**. For example, in a study by **Benschop et al**, men tend to experience changes in blood pressure, whereas women tended to display an increase in cardiac output and heart rate in response to severe stress **(290)**. During times of stress, heart rate can increase dramatically from a resting rate of about 70-80 beats per minute to over 150 beats per minute and vasoconstriction (narrowing of the blood vessels) results in an increase in blood pressure. *Changes to the cardiovascular system are one of the most easily recognizable effects to life's stresses.*

Finally, stress, particularly prolonged or persistent stress, may have a negative effect on the immune system. The immune system is the body's natural defense system that protects the body against foreign bodies (antigens), such as viruses. When the immune system is weakened, the ability of the body to fight disease is compromised. Stressors also result in a release of another type of hormone: corticosteroids. Corticosteroids are a class of hormones that reduce the effectiveness of the immune system to deal with foreign bodies by reducing the number of white blood cells, lymphocytes, which help the body to fight infections. Research also suggests that there may be a connection between continual stress and disease. Studies by **Cohen et al**, and **Levy et al**, reported higher rates of cancer and infections in stressed populations. *While the debate regarding stress and immunology will no doubt continue, many people assert that reducing stress is a first important step towards maintaining a healthy body.*

In conclusion, stress is an unavoidable part of life and can have both detrimental and beneficial effects on performance and health. The feeling of being stressed is not only a psychological response to a condition or context but a biological reaction that is easily measureable. When stressed, people may exhibit an urge to escape or face a situation head on as the hormonal response

kicks in. A pounding heart and heightened blood pressure are the first tell-tale signs of stress. Finally, while stressful feelings may subside as quickly as they came, if left unattended, health and vitality may be reduced and the risk of disease may increase. As stress becomes a more common and permanent feature in the lives of many people, understanding its effect on the body is essential in order to combat its negative effects.

Activity 2

Go back through the essay and look at the parts of the essay that are highlighted. These highlighted parts are important components of an academic essay and will be explained in this section of the book.

The Introductory Paragraph

The introductory paragraph in an essay does three things:

1. **Introduce the topic**

2. **Show the structure of the essay**, often with the major sections of the essay or its structural principle clearly stated.

3. **State the thesis of the essay**, preferably in a single statement with a clear main clause.

The introductory paragraph consists of three parts:

Hook(s) + Background Information + Thesis Statement = Introductory Paragraph

What is a thesis statement?

The thesis statement is a road map for the essay; it tells the reader what to expect from the rest of the essay.

The thesis statement is similar to a topic sentence in that it serves to control or shape the text. The thesis statement, like a topic sentence, contains a **topic** (T) and **controlling idea(s)** (CI). However, with the thesis statement, the T and CI influence the whole essay.

In this sense, a thesis statement is like a "super-topic sentence."

There are some differences, however, between a topic sentence and a thesis statement:

- A thesis statement is usually the **final sentence** in the introductory paragraph
- A thesis statement may list subtopics, which are smaller topics that relate to the main topic that will be expanded upon in the body paragraphs

Direct and Indirect Thesis Statements

A thesis statement can be direct or indirect. A direct thesis statement contains subtopics and therefore gives a specific outline of the essay.

Indirect thesis statement	There are considerable benefits of learning English for Korean students.
Direct thesis statement	For Korean people, learning English is important for three reasons: to gain entrance to good universities, improve job prospects, and open social opportunities.

Direct Thesis Statement

Example: In order for Sungkyunkwan University to become the leading university in Korea, three areas need to be reformed: the university **scholarship and welfare system**, the **administrative system**, and the **system of hiring faculty**.

This sentence tells the reader what the essay is going to be about (i.e. what Sungkyunkwan University needs to do to become the best university in Korea) and provides a structural outline for the body paragraphs.

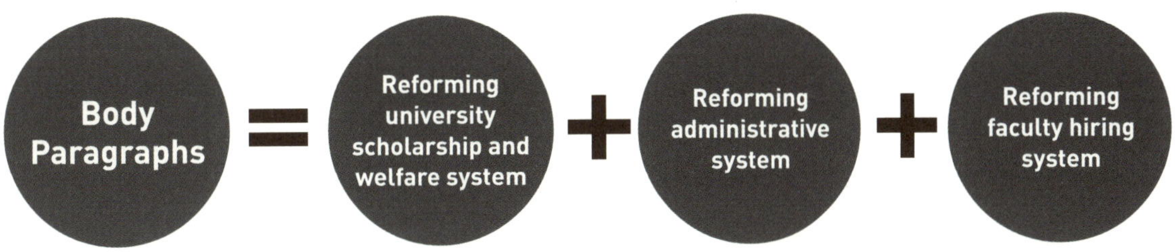

Activity 1

Read the following introduction, and answer the questions.

Today, smoking is an issue that is on everybody's mind. The whole country is divided on this issue. Some people believe that smoking should be banned everywhere while others are not so harsh. While it is true that smokers have rights too, tobacco should be outlawed because smoking endangers everyone's health, pollutes the environment, and drains people of valuable energy.

1. What is the thesis statement? Underline it.

2. How many subtopics are there? Underline them.

3. What do you think the rest of the essay will be about?

   a. The history of tobacco

   b. Why smoking is a bad habit

   c. Why tobacco should be banned (prohibited)

   d. How smoking divides the country

Punctuation Tip Colons (:)

Colons are used to introduce a list of items. They can be particularly helpful when writing thesis statements because they allow the writer to introduce the subtopics. Colons must be preceded by an independent clause.

IC

Example: Living in a city has certain advantages over living in town: more employment opportunities, better medical facilities, and higher educational standards. colon

Activity 2

Make the following into direct thesis statements by adding subtopics to them.

Computers are necessary for university students for three reasons

____

____

Successful K-pop groups have the following qualities

____

____

Students have a difficult time taking notes in class due to

____

____

To gain an internship in a prestigious Korean company requires

____

____

There are several reasons why the South Korean government should invest in education

____

____

There are three negative consequences for the population explosion in Seoul

____

____

Indirect Thesis Statement

An indirect thesis statement does not contain subtopics; however, the topic is still clearly stated.

Example: In order for Sungkyunkwan University to become the leading university in Korea, three areas need to be reformed.

What makes a good thesis statement?

A good thesis statement usually has at least one of the following attributes:

1. Takes a stance or position on a topic

Good example:
There are three reasons why smoking should be banned in all public places in Korea.

Poor example: **Does not give an opinion.**
A lot of people smoke in Korea.

2. Expresses one idea

Good example:
Shakespeare is considered one of the most influential figures in literary history.

Poor example: **Expresses more than one idea.**
Shakespeare is considered an important literary figure, and he was born in Stratford-upon-Avon which is a beautiful town in England.

3. It should be clear and specific

Good example:
Michael Jackson possessed all the qualities of a pop icon: incredible dancing skills, great vocal ability, and a commanding stage presence.

Poor example: **Is too broad.**
Michael Jackson is very famous.

4. Answers the question "Why?"

Good example: (Answers the question, "Why is the adoption rate in the United States increasing?)
Adoption rates in the United States are increasing due to incentive programs, positive campaigns, and fertility issues.

Poor example: **Does not answer "Why?"**
Researchers understand why the adoption rate in the United States is increasing.

Activity 3

Look at the following thesis statements. For each one, state whether it is a good thesis statement or a poor one. Give a reason for your view. If the thesis statement is poor, change it to make it better.

1. Learning English has some negative and positive aspects.

2. Korean companies need to enhance new technologies to increase sales, and they also need to change their marketing strategies.

3. There are many causes and effects of global warming.

4. *Buchaechum*, a traditional Korean form of dance, is a vital part of Korean culture and should therefore be taught to all female high school students.

5. Natural disasters, such as earthquakes and tsunamis, are something people should get used to.

General Statements

Making a good first impression is important when writing the introductory paragraph. The opening statements in an introductory paragraph should help to capture the attention of the reader as well as introduce the general topic of the essay.

In the introductory paragraph, the general statements precede the thesis statement and are made up of devices called a "**hook**" and "**background information**."

Hook

A hook is an interesting statement that helps to engage the readers by capturing their attention. There are many different kinds of hooks that can be used to start an introduction. Be aware that not every type of hook will work for every style of writing.

1. Interesting fact

A surprising fact, figure, or statistic can be a great way to draw interest in the topic. It can help the reader to focus on your main essay idea and can serve as a bridge for further supporting details in the body.

Example:

The city of Seoul has seen massive population changes over the last century and now accounts for almost half of the population of South Korea. **It is estimated that the Seoul National Capital Area has around 25 million inhabitants and is second only behind Tokyo in terms of world metropolitan figures.** While this population boom has been a key reason for the economic development of Seoul, and indeed South Korea, it has also had negative effects. There are three main negative consequences of the population explosion in Seoul.

2. Setting the Scene

This type of hook uses descriptive language to create a "picture" for your reader. It may describe how someone or something looks, smells, feels, or tastes and is useful in helping the reader connect with the topic you will introduce.

Example:

The buildings and houses lay scattered and in ruins. The night air is filled with the cries of people and the sirens of the emergency vehicles trying to navigate through the broken streets. People wander in a daze picking up personal items from the debris that used to be their houses. The chaos and destruction is overwhelming and tells a story of the awesome power of nature. An earthquake has struck. Earthquakes are one of the most devastating forces known to humanity because of a number of terrifying effects: shaking and ground rupture, tsunamis, and soil liquefaction.

3. Question

Asking a question in the introductory paragraph can help create an attachment between the reader and the writer. To strengthen the effect of the question, it is better to avoid yes/no questions or directly ask the reader a question (Do you like chocolate? Do you know Kim, Tae Hee?). Writers are meant to answer questions for readers. Therefore, writers should only use thought provoking questions that help to transition from one section or point to another. In addition, questions should be used sparingly.

Example:

Today, in the United States of America, heart disease is the number one cause of death and a major cause of disability. It is estimated that about every 30 seconds, an American will have some kind of coronary event. A healthy lifestyle and diet are seen as the best weapons against heart disease and yet, for many Americans, confusion still exists regarding what they should or should not consume. Most people already know that reducing saturated and trans fatty acids is an important first step; however, **what other dietary choices should people make?** Surprisingly, recent research has shown that the following three beverages have an effect on reducing the risk of heart disease: coffee, red wine, and beer.

4. Definition

A definition hook is used when the writer wishes to explain a difficult or unknown term that will be used throughout the essay.

Example:

For many visitors in China, the sight of Chinese people sitting around a table thoughtfully placing small tiles on a board is as much a part of the Chinese experience as visiting the Great Wall. The animated discussions and sounds of slapping tiles are signs that an intense game of Mahjong is taking place. **Mahjong is a traditional Chinese board game commonly played by four people. It is played with 136 tiles based on Chinese characters and symbols, and the object is to build sets by drawing and discarding tiles.** Once positions at the table have been finalized, there are three important steps involved in playing Mahjong: dealing the tiles, drawing the tiles, and building and breaking the wall.

5. Anecdote

An anecdote is a short story or personal account of a person, place, incident, or event that can be used to illustrate the ideas you want to make in your essay. Anecdotes are usually interesting and amusing and are based on real incidences.

Example:

Every day as a young boy, Edison "Edson" Arantes do Nascimento would walk down to the local school with his friends and kick an old leather ball around the concrete playground. When alone and without a ball, a sock stuffed with old newspapers tied at the top would suffice. Playing barefoot while kicking an old sock around the streets of Sao Paulo, Brazil never seemed to trouble the young man. He dreamed of a greater future. Early life was not easy for the hopeful young soccer star, and yet through the desperation and the difficulties, Edison Arantes do Nascimento rose to the top to become the greatest soccer player of all: Pelé.

6. Funnel

This type of hook is like a funnel because it is wide at the top and narrow at the bottom. It starts with general opening statements about the topic and gradually becomes narrower and more focused. The funnel finishes with a specific statement that can lead the reader into the thesis statement.

Example:

According to research by the Organization for Economic Cooperation and Development (OECD), South Korea is now ranked third among OECD countries with respect to divorce. The surging divorce rate is of great concern to family planning and welfare organizations, and the government has now been pulled into the issue as the problems caused by divorce begin to escalate. In order to navigate through this social transition, an understanding of the causes of divorce should be examined. Perhaps then some solutions can be found. There are three main reasons that can account for the high divorce rate in modern Korean society: the change in women's status in society, shift from collectivism to individualism, and a change in values regarding divorce.

Activity 4

Go back through each example introductory paragraph and underline the thesis statement. Which ones are direct thesis statements? Which ones are indirect?

Direct: ______________________________

Indirect: ______________________________

Now look at the following thesis statements (ThS). For each one, add a hook(s).

1. ______________________________

____

____

____

____

____

____

ThS: In most occupations, women are still unequal to men in three areas: salary, power, and status.

2. ____

____

____

____

____

____

____

ThS: Living in a dormitory offers several advantages to first-year students.

Choose two of the thesis statements from Activity 2, and add a hook(s).

3. ____

____

____

____

____

____

____

ThS: ____

4. ____

____

____

____

____

____

____

ThS: ____

Background Information

It is often necessary to provide some kind of bridge to connect the hook(s) and the thesis statement. Providing some background information helps the reader understand what the topic is about. Although it may appear from the flow diagram on page 54 that background information comes between the hook and the thesis statement, it can come before the hook, after the hook, or both. Together the two parts make up the general statements. Consider the following two examples.

Example 1:

The city of Seoul has seen massive population changes over the last century and now accounts for almost half of the population of South Korea. **It is estimated that the Seoul National Capital Area has around 25 million inhabitants and is second only behind Tokyo in terms of world metropolitan figures.** While this population boom has been a key reason for the economic development of Seoul, and indeed South Korea, it has also had negative effects as well. There are three main negative consequences of the population explosion in Seoul.

The hook is in bold. The thesis statement is the last sentence. The underlined information serves to frame the hook and thesis statement. We call this background information.

In Example 2, there are two different kinds of hooks. What are they?

1. ______________________________

2. ______________________________

Example 2:

In the United States of America today, heart disease is the number one cause of death and is a major cause of disability. It is estimated that about every 30 seconds, an American will have some kind of coronary event. A healthy lifestyle and diet is seen as the best weapons against heart disease and yet for many Americans, confusion still exists regarding what they should or should not consume. Most people already know that reducing saturated and trans fatty acids is an important first step; however, what other dietary choices should people make? Surprisingly, recent research has shown that the following three beverages have an effect on reducing the risk of heart disease: coffee, red wine, and beer.

Activity 5

Look at the following topics. For each one, write a clear thesis statement (either direct or indirect), and then add some general statements.

Topic: School examinations

Topic: University

Topic: Learning a language

The Body Paragraphs

In the five-paragraph model essay, the body consists of three paragraphs. Each paragraph develops a subdivision of the topic that is described in the thesis statement. Like supporting sentences in a paragraph, each body paragraph helps to develop and support the main idea of the essay.

Each body paragraph usually contains these three parts:

1. A topic sentence
2. Supporting details
3. A concluding sentence

If you have used a direct thesis statement in your introductory paragraph, each subtopic will form the main theme in each body paragraph. Each main idea can then be examined and described in more detail. If you have used an indirect thesis statement, then suitable ideas will need to be created. This will usually take place during pre-writing and will form part of the essay outline.

Example:

Responding to Stress

The term "stress" is often used to describe the feelings of being overloaded and overwhelmed with the changes and demands of life. Sheldon Cohen et al, in their book *Measuring Stress*, describe stress as the process in which "environmental demands tax or exceed the adaptive capacity of an organism, resulting in psychological and biological changes" (3). These biological changes may be immediate and temporal as well as long term and constant, and can have both positive and negative effects. When measuring the effects of stress on the body, it is common to discuss three biological responses: the **hormonal response**, the **cardiovascular response**, and the **immune response**.

Body Patterns and Organization

Depending on the type of essay you are writing, different patterns or organizational structures are used. These patterns will be explained in more detail later in the book when you examine "Types of Writing." In the meantime, we will work on a basic 3-step paragraph structure.

Step 1: Create a topic sentence

Step 2: Give support for the idea you wish to develop

Step 3: Complete the paragraph with a concluding sentence

Introductory paragraph	**Thesis statement**: When measuring the effects of stress on the body, it is common to discuss three biological responses: the **hormonal response**, the **cardiovascular response**, and the **immune response**.
B1: Hormonal response	• Clear topic sentence • Supporting details that discuss and/or provide evidence for **the hormonal response** • A clear concluding sentence
B2: Cardiovascular response	• Clear topic sentence • Supporting details that discuss and/or provide evidence for the **cardiovascular response** • A clear concluding sentence
B3: Immune response	• Clear topic sentence • Supporting details that discuss and/or provide evidence for **the immune response** • A clear concluding sentence
Concluding paragraph	• The explanation for concluding paragraphs begins on page 76

Supporting Details

The supporting details in each body paragraph must clearly relate to that paragraph's topic sentence. There are a number of different kinds of supporting details.

Description	Soil liquefaction commonly occurs during earthquakes and result in the soil losing its strength and stiffness. Consequently, it effectively turns into "quicksand," causing structural failures in towns and cities.
Definition	Soil liquefaction is defined as the transformation from a solid state to a liquid state as a consequence of increased pressure and stress (Gutani 138).
Examples	English is widely used by many Korean professors as the principal means of instruction. For example, according to Incheon University's website, 36% of Korean professors now use English in the classroom (Kim 29).
Statistics/figure	According to statistics from a recent Gallup poll, Korean parents in Seoul spend 200,000 won a month on average on private English tuition (Shirazi 3).
Fact	Sungkyunkwan University was founded in 1398 and is the oldest university in East Asia.
Quotation	On the topic of customer service, Rolf Bauer, Chief Executive of Neo Heavy Industry Korea (NHIK), said, "It is vital for our customers to understand that when we make a promise, we deliver" (Dennison 19).

Activity 6

For each of the following thesis statements, select one subtopic and provide supporting details.

1. Tobacco should be outlawed because smoking endangers everyone's health, pollutes the environment, and drains people of valuable energy.

Body idea: ______________________

Supporting details: ______________________

____

____

____

____

____

2. Living in a city has certain advantages over living in a town: better entertainment options, greater employment opportunities, and more efficient transportation.

Body idea: ______________________

Supporting details: ______________________

____

____

____

____

____

3. The computer gaming boom is a serious problem in South Korea for three reasons: it can lead to addiction, cause physical health problems, and lead to anti-social behavior.

Body idea: ______________________

Supporting details: ______________________

____

____

____

____

Activity 7

From the following indirect thesis statement, create three body paragraphs following the 3-step approach.

Step 1: Create a topic sentence

Step 2: Give support for the idea you wish to develop

Step 3: Complete the paragraph with a concluding sentence

ThS: Living in a dormitory offers several advantages to first-year students.

B1 Topic sentence: ______________________________

____

____

Supporting details: ______________________________

____

____

____

____

____

____

____

Concluding sentence: ______________________________

____

____

____

Body Paragraph Transitions

It was mentioned on page 36 that good writing must have unity. That is, the ideas in the paragraph should all support each other. In order to achieve unity across paragraphs, transitional words and phrases are necessary. Transition words are signposts that provide signals to the reader on the organizational structure of an essay.

When used in an essay, transitions usually precede the independent clause; thus, they are commonly found at the beginning of a body or concluding paragraph. Transition words are usually followed by a comma.

Example 1:
First, reforming the university scholarship and welfare system is a vital step in helping Sungkyunkwan University become a leader in education.
Second, reforming the administrative system is also very important.
Finally, changing the faculty hiring system is necessary to ensure that high standards are kept.

Example 2:
Reforming the university scholarship and welfare system is a vital step in helping Sungkyunkwan University become a leader in education.
In addition to reforming the scholarship and welfare system, changes to the administrative system are vitally important.
Lastly, a change to the faculty hiring system is necessary to ensure high standards are kept.

Common Transition Words

Transitions that indicate time or sequence	first, second, third, next, finally, lastly
Transitions that indicate more information	next, in addition, furthermore, similarly, in the same way, also, moreover
Transitional chains	• First..second..third • In the first place...also..lastly • In the first place...just the same way...finally

B2 Topic sentence: ____

____

____

Supporting details: ____

____

____

____

____

____

____

____

Concluding sentence: ____

____

____

B3 Topic sentence: ____

____

____

Supporting details: ____

____

____

____

____

____

____

____

Concluding sentence: ____

____

____

The Concluding Paragraph

The final paragraph in an essay is the conclusion. Along with the introductory paragraph, it helps to frame your essay. In some respects, the concluding paragraph is like a mirror image of your introductory paragraph.

Introductory paragraph

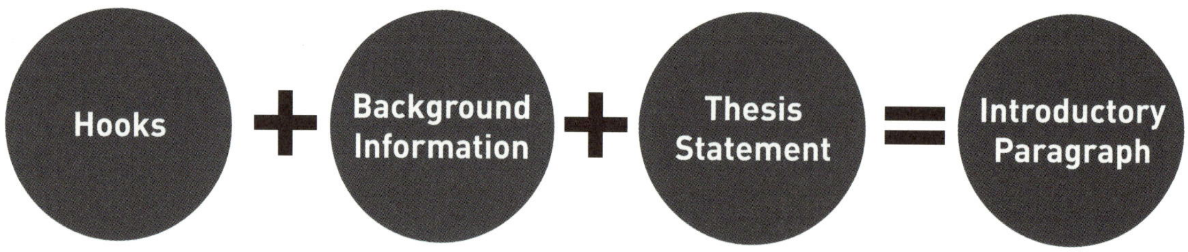

Concluding paragraph

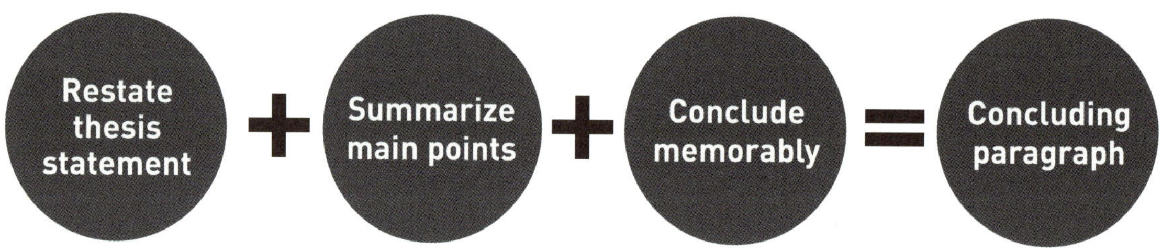

Like your body paragraphs, the concluding paragraph usually begins with a transition. Next, the writer **restates** the thesis statement found in the introductory paragraph and then **summarizes** the ideas in the main body. Finally, we can use a **reverse hook** to leave the reader with an interesting final thought.

Restating the Thesis Statement

By restating the thesis statement, the concluding paragraph can be connected to the introductory paragraph. We make this connection by paraphrasing the thesis statement.

Page 166 covers paraphrasing and summarizing. The two basic rules for effective paraphrasing are:

1. Find synonyms
2. Change the sentence structure or word order

Example 1: James loves going to the mountains, but Sarah loves to swim.
1. James likes hiking, but Sarah enjoys swimming.
2. Sarah enjoys swimming, but James likes hiking.

Example 2: Thesis statement

Living in a large city has certain advantages over living in a small town: better entertainment options, greater employment opportunities, and more efficient transportation.

Restatement of the thesis statement:
1. It is better to live in a large city than a small town for the following reasons: more interesting things to do, greater job flexibility, easier to commute to places.
2. Citizens who live in large cities have more choices with regard to entertainment and culture. In addition, it is easier to get a job, and the transportation is more convenient. It is clear then, that living in a large city is better.

Activity 1

Rewrite the following thesis statements using the basic paraphrasing steps.

Earthquakes are one of the most devastating forces known to humanity because of a number of terrifying effects: shaking and ground rupture, tsunamis, and soil liquefaction.

____

____

____

Signpost See page 166 for more information on paraphrasing.

Surprisingly, recent research has shown that the following three beverages have an effect on reducing the risk of heart attack: coffee, red wine, and beer.

____

____

____

There are three important steps involved in playing Mahjong once positions at the table have been finalized: building and breaking the wall, dealing the tiles, and drawing the tiles.

____

____

____

Summarizing the Main Points

If you have used an indirect thesis statement, a brief summary of the main points is recommended. This will remind the reader of the key ideas in your essay. Even if you have restated a direct thesis statement, a summary of the main points can still be worthwhile. You do not need to re-tell all the information; a few sentences are often enough.

Example:
ThS: There are three main negative consequences of the population explosion in Seoul.

B1: More traffic congestion and delays in travel

B2: An increase in air, soil, and noise pollution

B3: Increasing cost of living

In conclusion, it can be seen that the massive population growth in Seoul in the last thirty years has resulted in a number of negative factors. As the population has grown, the number of cars on the road has increased proportionately. The burden on the public transportation system is leading to longer delays in travel time which can then lead to rising stress levels. In addition, the growing pollution rate is a major concern for Seoul's inhabitants. Finally, with a greater demand in housing, prices are soaring across the city.

Activity 2

Look at the following thesis statements and details in the body. Paraphrase the thesis statement and add summary points.

Early life was not easy for the hopeful young soccer star, and yet, through the desperation and the difficulties, Edison Arantes do Nascimento rose to the top to become the greatest soccer player of all, Pelé.

B1: Living in poverty

B2: Hard work and dedication to soccer

B3: Becoming the best player in the world and winning the World Cup

____

____

____

____

____

____

English is a key that unlocks many opportunities, and for this reason, learning English is an important goal for most Korean students.

B1: Many prestigious universities in Korea use English as the language of instruction and teaching.

B2: Many companies in Korea now require employees to have a strong English ability.

B3: English allows students to travel with confidence and communicate with people in other countries.

____

____

____

____

____

____

____

Conclude Memorably

Just as a hook helps to engage the readers by capturing their attention, the final sentences in the concluding paragraph can leave the reader with an interesting thought on the topic.

1. Make a prediction: What do you think will happen in the future?

> Tuition fees at Korean universities have been rising while at the same time, financial aid for students has been declining. **If this trend continues, fewer and fewer families will be able to send their children to university.**

2. Recommend an action to be followed (call to action): Making a final statement that advises an action to be taken can leave the reader with a strong impression with the reader. This is commonly used in persuasive writing.

> The cost of attending university in Korea has been increasing. Students are finding the financial strain to be too much with many dropping out of school. It is clear that the Korean system of higher education is in trouble. **To reverse this trend, students must demand that the government increase its financial support for universities and improve financial aid programs.**

3. End with a warning: What are the consequences of not taking action?

> With costs rising and financial aid declining, Korean university students are now facing a crisis with many dropping out or going to other countries to study. If Korea is to prosper in the future, the brightest young minds cannot be lost. **Without a change to the current system, Korea will not maintain its current position as a major economic power in Asia.**

4. Ask a provocative question: Engaging the reader by posing an interesting question is a great way to make a strong final impression.

> As people live much longer through the advancement of technology and better nutrition, the issues regarding adequate medical care becomes increasingly important. This is a situation that affects everyone and is an issue that people cannot ignore any longer. Society must approach this issue with great care and consideration. **What will the aging population do?**

5. Use a final quotation: Like an opening quote in a hook, a final quotation that ties in with the main idea is also a good method for creating a strong ending.

With costs rising and financial aid declining, Korean university students are now facing a crisis. If Korea is to prosper in the future, Koreans cannot let their brightest young minds be lost. **As Kim, Sang Jun argued in his book, *The Future Starts Now*, "A nation's economic wealth will increase through an educated public"** (Kim 121). It is therefore imperative that students be given a "fair-go" so that they may build a better Korea.

Activity 3

In the following examples, the writer has restated the thesis statement and summarized the main point. Now add a memorable conclusion.

Citizens of large cities have more choices with regard to entertainment and culture. In addition, it is easier to get a job, and the transportation is also more convenient. It is clear that living in a large city is better.

____

____

____

____

____

In conclusion, the massive population growth in Seoul in the last thirty years has resulted in a number of negative factors. As the population has grown, the number of cars on the road has increased proportionately. The burden on the public transportation system is leading to longer delays in travel time, which can then lead to rising stress levels. In addition, increasing pollution is choking the city and is a major concern for Seoul's inhabitants. Finally, with a greater demand in housing, prices are soaring across the city.

____

____

____

____

____

For many Korean students, learning English is vital in opening the door to opportunity. Having strong English language background can make university life easier and can help students to gain access to the best jobs after they graduate. In addition, it can also make travel easier and more enjoyable.

What to Avoid in Your Conclusion

Never apologize or make a personal comment to the reader.

Example:

With costs rising and financial aid declining, Korean university students are now facing a crisis. If Korea is to prosper in the future, it is important to avoid losing the brightest young minds. **Sorry for my bad English. I tried my best ㅠㅠ.**

The conclusion is not the place to bring up new ideas.

Example:

With costs rising and financial aid declining, Korean university students are now facing a crisis. If Korea is to prosper in the future, we cannot let our brightest young minds be lost. **Korean universities also need to help students more by providing better research and study facilities.**

Do not finish with a sentimental or emotional statement.

Example:

As people live longer because of science and better nutrition, there will be greater problems in the future with an aging population. This is a situation that affects everyone and society cannot ignore it any longer. **I hope in the future that all the elderly people in the world can live happy lives.**

Activity 4

Read the three body paragraphs, and then add an introductory and concluding paragraph.

First, daily homework is important because it can help students to reinforce lecture notes. It is often difficult for students to understand everything in a lecture. Students are often tired, and it can be difficult to understand teachers. Therefore, homework is an important tool to reinforce classroom content. If students do not understand the content of the lectures during class time, it is easy for them to fall behind. To ensure that students keep up with the content of a lecture, doing homework is important.

While doing homework is important for reinforcing in-class learning, homework can also expose students to different ideas by giving them extra information not covered in class. At university, it is important for students to broaden their knowledge, but this is not always possible during class time. Due to time constraints, teachers cannot always cover everything about a topic. Therefore, in order to provide students with new ideas on a topic, teachers can give homework to their students.

Another strong argument for the necessity of homework is that it gives students the opportunity to share their own ideas. During university lectures, students do not always have the chance to voice their own opinions. In many lectures, students are simply passive learners only taking in the information given to them from the professors. By doing homework however, students can have a chance to apply classroom content and provide answers to questions. In this sense, homework can give students the opportunity to put forward their own ideas, which can enhance learning.

Styles of Writing

While there are very general types of writing (sentences, paragraphs, essays), there are also more specific styles of writing that are used in different contexts. After learning the basics of sentences, paragraphs, and essays, this section will help writers to refine their skills and tailor their writing to particular circumstances. Each subsection covers a style of writing, gives an example of the style (paragraph, essay, or paragraph and essay), and helps students to understand how to perfect each form through various activities (topic selection, brainstorming, structure, outlining, and/or connecting words).

This section starts with personal writing to help students express and structure information about their life in written form. The following subsection develops students' ability to accurately and creatively describe things through writing. Finally, the last four styles are more academic, and these forms of writing will prepare students to write in a university environment.

This section covers:

- Personal Statement
- Descriptive Writing
- Classification Writing
- Compare and Contrast Writing
- Cause and Effect Writing
- Persuasive Writing

1 Personal Statement

A personal statement is your opportunity to sell yourself to the reader. Whenever you apply for a work, study, or apprenticeship position, there is a very strong chance that you will be required to write a personal statement as part of the application process. The purpose is to provide evidence and context for the rest of the information in your application, giving you the opportunity to go beyond the basic required information and show more of yourself to the reader. In most cases, the person reading your personal statement will not have met you before, and all they have to go on is the basic information on your application form. It is, therefore, a very important first opportunity to share your personality, aims, successes, and what makes you who you are.

A good personal statement:

- Refers to information given in other parts of the application, adding clarity, depth, and context.
- Makes a strong case for admission or invitation to interview by showcasing relevant skills as well as your personality.

A good starting point is to think of a few words to describe yourself. This can give a clear, simple foundation on which you can build later. Words with more than one positive meaning can be especially powerful. Avoid very simple or bland words such as "happy," "good," or "nice," and instead think of words that show particular strengths in your personality and character.

Activity 1

Read the sentences in the box below. Each one relates to an adjective which describes a quality of the writer. For each example, choose the most appropriate adjective. Which adjectives should the writer avoid using? Why?

I am...

___________ – I am highly self-motivated, enjoy challenges, and I work hard to achieve goals. For example, as a freshman, I organized, promoted, and ran a food stall at the school's spring festival that raised over ₩500,000.

___________ – I work well with others. For example, during my senior year at high school I worked as part of a team to arrange a series of events for visiting foreign students.

___________ – I am quick thinking and good at finding solutions to problems. For instance, I am often trusted to close the restaurant at which I work part-time. On one occasion there was a fire in the kitchen, and I dealt with this situation efficiently with no harm to anyone.

Capable, independent, challenged, dynamic, cooperative, tough, extraordinary, lewd, peaceful, buoyant, smart, flexible, determined, professional, logical, tolerant, amorous

Tip

A thesaurus is a great tool for increasing your vocabulary and finding alternative or more impressive ways to make a point. Remember to always use your thesaurus in conjunction with a dictionary to make sure of the meaning of the words you find. They may be similar to your original word but not necessarily the same. Make sure your words carry the message you want the reader to receive.

For example
Dynamic: energetic, motivated, forceful, aggressive, adaptable, changing

Activity 2

In your notebook, brainstorm a short list of words that describe you. Check the meanings of the words and see if there are any that you could change to more interesting or effective synonyms.

Pick the three words that best describe your most positive characteristics, and add them to the boxes below. Write a sentence or two to explain each word and give evidence for each characteristic.

I am...	Explanation and evidence/example
1.________________	________________________________ ________________________________ ________________________________
2.________________	________________________________ ________________________________ ________________________________
3.________________	________________________________ ________________________________ ________________________________

Remember: These are the qualities which you want to showcase in your personal statement. They are the main points that you want the reader to learn about you and what you want them to remember after reading your statement.

A Basic Personal Statement

Once you have defined your qualities with three descriptive words, you can think about writing your statement. Remember, if your personal statement is part of an application, it should be the last thing that you complete and should support the facts that make up the rest of the application.

Activity 3

Write an appropriate topic sentence and concluding sentence to make the personal statement into a complete paragraph.

Personal Statement

____

____

First of all, I am dynamic. I am highly self-motivated, enjoy challenges, and I work hard to achieve goals. For example, as a freshman, I organized, promoted, and ran a food stall at the school's spring festival that raised over ₩500,000. I am also cooperative. For instance, during my senior year at high school I worked as part of a team to arrange a series of events for visiting foreign students, giving them a great experience of Seoul and an understanding of what it means to be Korean. Finally, I am resourceful and good at finding solutions to problems. For example, I am often trusted to close the restaurant at which I work part-time. On one occasion, there was a fire in the kitchen, and I dealt with this situation efficiently with no harm to anyone.

____

____

Activity 4

In your notebook, use your information from Activity 2 to plan and write a one paragraph personal statement that describes your strongest qualities. Remember to think about your academic career so far. Since you are so close to this account, it can be hard to adjust your perspective. Try to be objective and consider the significant moments and achievements. Some of your accomplishments and experiences might seem ordinary to you, but try to consider them from another perspective. What do they say about you? What skills, characteristics or qualities do they reveal? How have these experiences made you who you are today?

Personal Statements Using Prompts

In most situations in which you might need to write a personal statement, including most application forms, a prompt will be provided. This prompt tells the writer what information to include in their statement.

A prompted personal statement usually focuses on one of three areas, which can be phrased as questions in order to make the writing task easier to follow:

- What is your background and how has it shaped you into who you are today?
- What characteristics and skills can you contribute to your chosen area of study or work?
- What abilities or accomplishments demonstrate your best qualities?

Remember:

Read the instructions: There may well be instructions for your personal statement, such as prompts or areas on which to focus. There may also be instructions on how much to write. For example, a paragraph, at least 250 words, no more than 1,000 words, a short essay. Read the instructions carefully and always follow them. Your statement will be useless if it does not meet the requirements.

Think about the purpose: What is the purpose of the application? What does the reader want/need to know about you? Try to anticipate questions they might have, such as evidence of specific skills or qualities required for a job, interest and ability in a subject you wish to study, or more general skills that might benefit you and your department in your chosen field of study. Make sure you give specific experiences and explain how they have made you who you are.

Tip

Words to Avoid:

- Flexible – empty, meaningless, can sound desperate
- Determined – sounds like always trying but never achieving a leadership role
- Professional – used by self-promoters with nothing worth promoting
- Logical – everyone thinks they are
- Tolerant – not necessarily positive (can be tolerant of bad behaviour)
- Creative – empty-sounding
- Experienced – your application form will show your experience
- Efficient – meaningless
- Competent – sounds like you are not an expert
- Ambitious – evident in your application, can sound negative.
- Reliable –all workers should be reliable

Activity 5

Read the prompt and example personal statement below and answer the following questions.

a) How does the writer describe his or her hometown?

b) How does the writer describe his or her family?

c) What issues did the writer face?

d) How did these situations affect the writer's character?

Prompt: What is your background (family, school, hometown)? How has it influenced your character?

Personal Statement

I am a confident person who enjoys new challenges. I spent most of my childhood in Uljin, which is a small coastal town on the East coast of the Korean Peninsula. As an only child, I received a lot of attention from my parents, and this attention gave me a sense of great self-importance. It also gave me confidence and independence, which were fueled by regular trips to the beach and the mountains with my friends. Before starting high school, my family moved from our small familiar town to the bustling metropolis of Seoul. Until then I had been consistently at the top of my class, but suddenly I was faced with far greater competition. This was a shock at first, but it taught me humility to balance my strong confidence. In high school I studied incredibly hard, well aware of the stiff competition with which I was faced. My confident and outgoing nature helped me to make a lot of good friends. After taking the university placement test, we took a trip to China. Travelling in a foreign country for a month was a real adventure, and I relished every new experience. Growing up like this has helped my confident, outgoing character to develop.

Activity 6

Write one paragraph in response to the following prompt:
What is your background (family, school, hometown)? How has it influenced your character?

Before writing your paragraph, think about:

- How you might describe your family, school, or hometown?
- What major issue you have faced personally and how you dealt with them?
- How facing this issue has changed you?

Activity 7

Read the prompt and example personal statement below and answer the following questions.

a) What is the writer's major? How does he or she describe his or her interest in this subject?

b) How did the writer's childhood affect his or her choice of major?

c) What opportunities has the writer taken that are related to his or her major?

d) What practical experience does he or she have in his or her chosen field?

Prompt: What is your major? Why did you choose this subject, and how has your interest in the subject developed?

Personal Statement

I have been obsessed with fashion for as long as I can remember, and this has led to the very natural step of pursuing a degree in fashion design. As a young child, I was fascinated by the elegant garments my mother wore, and I would spend hours sketching pictures of myself in similar outfits. I was always convinced that I could improve on current designs, and I got into a lot of trouble for trying to "improve" one of my mother's favorite dresses. My family moved to Hong Kong when I was in middle school, and it was there that my ambition to become a designer really bloomed. The school put on an annual production of a famous play, and in my final year, we were to perform *Grease*. I was put in charge of wardrobe, which involved designing and making the costumes for the actors. The 1950's outfits were really inspiring, and the experience drove me on to delve deeper into the world of fashion. I attended many shows and exhibitions in Hong Kong. Since returning to Seoul, I have taken a part-time job at a boutique in Apgujeong, where I am continuing to learn. Fashion design is in my blood, and my fashion design major is the next important step in fulfilling my dream of becoming a successful designer.

Activity 8

Write one paragraph in response to the following prompt:

What is your major? Why did you choose this subject, and how has your interest in the subject developed?

Before writing your paragraph, think about:

- What influenced your choice of major?
- How does your choice of major reflect your personality?
- What events in your past may have influenced your choice of major?
- What opportunities related to your major have you taken?

Activity 9

Read the prompt and example personal statement below and answer the following questions.

a) What is the writer's achievement?
b) How does the writer describe his or her character?
c) What else does the writer's achievement tell you about his or her character?
d) How might this achievement impress an employer or admissions board?

Prompt: What accomplishment are you most proud of? Why are you proud of this accomplishment, and what does this say about your qualities and character?

Personal Statement

My greatest accomplishment demonstrates dedication, hard work, and taking on a challenge. When I was about to start high school my family adopted a dog from an elderly couple. The dog, a beagle, was quite old, bad tempered, and in poor condition, but he quickly became part of the family. I had never trained a dog before, and he had clearly never been trained, so I did a lot of research into how to teach an old dog new tricks. Throughout high school I worked with Pickles every day. After three years we had made great progress, but we had never entered a competition, so to test both of our abilities, we decided to enter Pickles into a show. We entered the show, and Pickles performed impeccably. Nobody could believe that he had been a rescue dog, or that he had only started training in his later years. While we did not win the contest, we managed to finish in second place in the obedience category. This is a demonstration of my commitment to a task, and my willingness to work hard.

Activity 10

Write a one paragraph response to the following prompt:
What accomplishment are you most proud of? Why are you proud of this accomplishment and what does this say about your qualities and character?

- What your strongest quality is and how you can describe this in a single word?
- What accomplishment best showcases this quality?
- How the accomplishment itself might affect the reader's opinion of you?
- What secondary qualities might shine through your accomplishment?

2 Descriptive Writing

Unlike other forms of writing found later in this section, descriptive writing is not a way to structure your writing. Instead, it is a style of writing that invokes the senses or provides more detail using adjectives, adverbs, and more precise vocabulary to paint a picture for your reader. In other words, writers do not tell their readers what something is; they show what they want to convey through their descriptions.

Descriptive writing is not usually used for formal academic writing. It is more often used in advertising and marketing campaigns to promote new or improved products, in tourism to attract tourists, and in narrative writing to build characters, setting, and atmosphere.

In this section you will:

- Examine two different descriptive paragraphs
- Learn to identify and build atmosphere through descriptive words
- Learn about the differences between connotation and denotation
- Identify the connotation and denotation of various words
- Practice describing objects using precise vocabulary
- Brainstorm for descriptive writing
- Write your own assignments using the tools you have developed in this section

Activity 1

Answer the following questions about places you have been.

1. Think about the best place you have visited. What words would you use to describe this place?
2. What was is the worst place you have visited? What words would you use to describe this place?

Descriptive Paragraph Example 1

Heaven on Earth

Paradise Beach is a fabulous place for a holiday. This private, secluded beach is an ideal place to spend a relaxing and peaceful vacation. For instance, this pristine area features kilometers of silky sand that is soft to lie on and warm on the toes. Stretching in front on the beach are the calm waters of the Pacific Ocean. Visitors relaxing on the beach enjoy the fragrant sea breeze while watching the waves gently lap and roll onto the sand. Later, when the sun rises high in the endless sky devoid of clouds, the ocean's clear waters become even more inviting and refreshing. Thus, as a vacation destination, no other beach can compare to this tranquil heavenly spot.

Descriptive Paragraph Example 2

Paradise Is Hell

Paradise Beach is a wretched place to take a vacation. Because of its isolation from other tourist areas and the dreadful natural surroundings, Paradise Beach is a desolate place. The sand is gritty and rough on sensitive toes, and the beach is littered with garbage from the dark waters of the Pacific Ocean. Even when a spot devoid of waste is found on the beach, holidaymakers rarely stay as the sweltering heat scorches the sand and makes it unbearable to relax. However, the menacing ocean brings no relief for overheated vacationers as the violent, crashing waves are enough to terrify even the most advanced swimmers. In addition, the putrid sea breeze warns of water polluted by waste, and the dull grey sky is menacing. Therefore, if travelers want a spot to experience heaven on Earth, Paradise Beach is the last place they should go for a blissful vacation.

Activity 2

Highlight the descriptive words used in the example paragraphs. Then fill in the following chart to see the differences in the words used to describe various nouns in the passages.

Noun	Paragraph 1	Paragraph 2
Beach/Area		
Sand		
Ocean/Waves		
Sea breeze		
Sky/Sun		

Activity 3

Choose another noun that you would find at a beach, and write it in the empty section of the chart above. Then think of several words you could use to describe the noun for both paragraphs. Afterward, write your own additional sentence in your notebook for each of these paragraphs by incorporating these descriptive words.

Connotation and Denotation

"Denotation" means the dictionary definition of a word while "connotation" refers to the emotional meaning; therefore, while two words have the same meaning, they do not always invoke the same feeling.

The government **brainwashed** its citizens into agreeing to the new law.
The government **persuaded** its citizens to agree with the new law.

Both words mean "finding a way to get another person to agree with an opinion;" however, "brainwashed" has a very negative connotation because it sounds irrational while "persuaded" means that people have become convinced through thoughtful arguments.

Activity 4

Complete the following passage by filling in your own words. Afterward, share your story with your classmates and see if there are any differences in your stories based on the words you chose.

The ____________ house with ________________ windows and a ____________ door was located on the corner of the ____________ street. It was surrounded by ____________ trees, _________________ flowers, and a ________________ gate. The house looked like it should be in a __________________ movie. From time to time, people would walk by the house and remark at how _______________ it looked. Although many people wanted to live there, in the end they decided against buying the property because it was _____________________.

Activity 5

Categorize the following words as negative or positive.

1. pushy, aggressive, assertive
2. curious, nosy, prying, inquisitive
3. lazy, leisurely, relaxing, slothful
4. youthful, immature, childish
5. unique, strange, weird, exceptional, distinctive, extraordinary
6. carefree, irresponsible, negligent, lax
7. rude, frank, honest, straightforward, candid, imprudent

Positive	Negative
1.	
2.	
3.	
4.	
5.	
6.	
7.	

Activity 6

Choose one of the following topics and brainstorm common nouns for that topic in the chart below. Afterwards, think about some positive and negative ways to describe each noun. It may help you to think about the following categories of words: sight, taste, sound, touch, smell, or characteristics.

1. A person you know
2. A historical person
3. The person sitting across from you on a blind date
4. A vacation destination (real or imagined)
5. A new restaurant
6. An apartment for sale
7. A pet
8. A newly discovered animal
9. A new electronic product
10. A new car

Noun	Positive	Negative

Activity 7

After brainstorming both positive and negative words for your topic, write two different paragraphs using these words. Then have your partner read your paragraphs, and highlight the words that convey positive or negative meaning.

Signpost See page 146 for more information on the order of adjectives. In general, you should not write more than three adjectives and a determiner before one noun.

3 Classification Writing

Classification writing is a way of organizing or sorting ideas or items into categories. In a classification paragraph or essay, the writer describes and develops ideas by sorting the contents into groups or classes. Classification is often used by scientists to show the relationship between living organisms. Dance or physical education students may need to use classification as a way to describe and analyze types of dance or sport. Classification is also utilized by businesses and individuals as a means of exploring market research or products. Classification writing can be used with almost any subject.

In this section you will:

- Examine a model classification paragraph and essay
- Analyze the organization of a classification essay
- Write a classification paragraph or essay

Activity 1

Complete the following questions and then read the essay.

1. Have you ever watched a television program or movie featuring a character that was a monster or mythical creature?
   Check the ones you have seen.

   ____ zombies ____ ghosts ____ vampires ____ dragons
   ____ aliens ____ werewolves ____ demons ____ sea monsters
   Other ____________________

2. If you were confronted by a vampire, zombie, or werewolf, what would you do?

Understanding the Threat

Monstrous and evil figures have existed in legend for thousands of years, and in the last century with the arrival of film and television the concept of the monster has been pushed further into the forefront of popular culture. In recent times a more romantic view of monsters and mythological figures has been portrayed. In the popular novel and movie *Twilight*, characters like Edward Cullen and Jacob Black are not seen as terrifying or gruesome but instead as sexy and charming. In the animation series *Shrek*, the large green ogre is a peaceful hero who falls in love with a princess. In reality, nothing could be further from the truth. Monsters are not cute, sexy, or cool, and they should be feared at all times. A healthy knowledge of the characteristics of certain monsters and mythological figures is not only advisable, but also necessary if people wish to live a long life.

Perhaps the most well-known and documented mythological being is the vampire. In her book *The Vampire as Numinous Experience*, author Beth E. McDonald describes vampires as being "undead creatures resembling living humans who feed on the living by drinking the victim's blood" (21). The modern day vampire is depicted as healthy on the surface, able to talk and pass as human, and usually possessing of extraordinary or supernatural powers. Vampires create others like them when they bite their victim. A common belief regarding transformation is that when a vampire bites or feeds on a human, a retrovirus in the saliva or blood transforms the human into a vampire. Vampires usually react negatively to religious objects and also folk remedies such as garlic, wild rose, and mountain ash. It is also widely believed that weapons of silver, exposure to direct sunlight, and impaling a vampire through the heart with a wooden stake will kill them. Therefore, vampires are one the most fearsome of all mythological figures, and preparation is vital if one wishes to retain the upper hand.

Another monster that has been popularized in film and television is the zombie. While vampires are often described as "the undead," zombies are regarded as "the living dead." Kyle William Bishop in his book *American Gothic Zombie* describes the zombie as a corpse raised from the dead with pale skin, a vacant stare, and a decomposing body (110). Although zombies may walk upright and appear human from a distance, they are essentially dead and have no developed brain functions. As a result, they "cannot process information, learn from their mistakes, act in their own self-interests, or even speak. Instead zombies act on instinct and drive alone" (110). Similar to the vampire, the zombie is able to transform its victim by biting and infecting the victim. In popular film and television, zombiism appears to be viral with the victim first dying from a zombie attack before rising from the dead. However, unlike their undead counterpart the vampire, zombies cannot be injured or destroyed by religious symbols or plants. A zombie can be beaten, stabbed, torn limb from limb, or shot but the body will still continue on its relentless pursuit of human flesh if the brain is still intact. Thus, the only sure way to kill a zombie is to destroy its already rotting brain.

Another mythological creature that strikes fear into the heart and mind is the werewolf. The werewolf, also known as a lycanthrope, is a beast able to change between human and wolf form. Cryptozoologist Peter Velps describes werewolves as large wolf-like creatures with superhuman strength and increased senses (27). The mythology surrounding the werewolf reveals there are two ways of becoming a werewolf. First, lycanthropy is a hereditary condition, so a child can be born a werewolf. Second, a person can be turned into a werewolf if they are bitten by one. Like the zombie, werewolves are thought not to be affected by religious symbols, but they can be repelled by the herbs wolfsbane and mountain ash. It is thought that the only way to kill a werewolf is with weapons of silver like a silver sword or a silver bullet. Once a suspected werewolf is killed, the wolf will transform into human form and die. Therefore, if the creature killed does not transform back into human form, run. The werewolf is still out there.

Monsters and evil creatures have been around for centuries. While most people dismiss the notion of the existence of monsters, there are still some believers. Film goers may have fallen in love with Edward Cullen, but it should always be remembered that a vampire is an extremely dangerous adversary and should never be underestimated. In the unlikely event of a zombie apocalypse, stay quiet and out of sight. Do not assume that friends and family members are what they seem. Werewolves are brutally strong and fast, so trying to escape on foot is useless. Plant some wolfsbane in apartment gardens and stay inside when there is a full moon. Frank Herbert the acclaimed science fiction author said, "The beginning of knowledge is the discovery of something we do not understand (1)." To be fully prepared for the unexplained, learn about it first. It might be the difference between life and death.

Activity 2

Some people believe that monsters are not just real, but may be actually living in our communities. If a classmate, friend, or family member were a type of monster, who would it be and what type? Why do you suspect this? Discuss with a partner.

Organization of a Classification Essay

Once a topic has been chosen, the organization of the essay is fairly easy. If the writer wishes to examine three places to visit in France, the essay will have three body paragraphs. Similarly, if the writer decides to look at four main features on a DSLR camera, the body will be comprised of four body paragraphs.

Parallel Paragraph Structure

In a classification essay each body paragraph should contain the same supporting details. In an essay on places to visit in France, if the writer examines things to see, accommodation, and places to eat in the city of Paris, then the same three features should be used when writing about the other two places in France.

Basic paragraph structure

Place

1. Sights
2. Accommodation
3. Food

1. Body Paragraph 1: Paris
   a. Supporting detail 1: Things to see
   b. Supporting detail 2: Accommodation
   c. Supporting detail 3: Places to eat

2. Body Paragraph 2: French Riviera
   a. Supporting detail 1: Things to see
   b. Supporting detail 2: Accommodation
   c. Supporting detail 3: Places to eat

3. Body Paragraph 1: Provence
   a. Supporting detail 1: Things to see
   b. Supporting detail 2: Accommodation
   c. Supporting detail3: Places to eat

Activity 3

Go back to the essay "Understanding the Threat." Does the body have parallel structure? What are the three features examined in the body paragraph?

a. Supporting detail 1: ______________________________

b. Supporting detail 2: ______________________________

c. Supporting detail 3: ______________________________

Activity 4

Choose one of the following topics and create a body outline for a classification essay.

1. Computer games
2. The different coffee shops in Hyehwa
3. Singers/bands
4. University majors

Body Paragraph 1: ______________________________

a. Supporting detail ______________________________

____

b. Supporting detail ______________________________

____

c. Supporting detail ______________________________

____

Body Paragraph 2: ______________________________

a. Supporting detail ______________________________

____

b. Supporting detail ______________________________

____

c. Supporting details ______________________________

____

Body Paragraph 3: ______________________________

a. Supporting detail ______________________________

____

b. Supporting detail ______________________________

____

c. Supporting detail ______________________________

____

Activity 5

Using the information from your body outline in Activity 4, write a full essay with introduction and conclusion in your notebook.

4 Compare and Contrast Writing

Compare and contrast writing takes two or more topics and examines their similarities, differences, or similarities and differences. Unlike persuasive writing, compare and contrast writing does not make a judgement or take a particular stance on how one topic is better or worse than the other. Rather, this type of writing looks at the topics objectively. However, even though you will be comparing or contrasting two or more different topics, you need to make sure that you still have one thesis statement. In addition, you should also give an approximately equal amount of space to both topics to ensure a balanced assignment.

Compare and contrast writing is often used in academic writing to objectively examine multiple topics or options. For example, students might look at two dynasties in a history class, different products in a business paper, or more than one styles of dance in a performing arts program. Nevertheless, employees may also use compare and contrast writing in a non-academic context in order to compare two different financial packages available at a bank or credit card company, explore two travel options for a tourist agency, or various course choices at a university.

In this section you will:

- Learn different kinds of compare and contrast structure
- Examine a compare and contrast essay
- Learn to identify good and bad topic combinations
- Practice Venn and T-Chart brainstorming
- Use compare and contrast connecting words
- Write your own compare and contrast assignment using the skills learned in this section

Activity 1

Answer the following questions about holidays.

1. What is your favorite holiday? What do you like most about this holiday?
2. How do you think traditional holidays like Chuseok and Seollal will change in fifty years?

Thanksgiving and Chuseok: Unique Festivals for Unique Cultures

Many cultures around the world hold festivals or celebrate special days devoted to being thankful for newly harvested food. In the United States of America, Thanksgiving, which is held on the 4th Thursday in November, is one of the most important holidays. Likewise, Koreans have a traditional festival held on the 15th day of the 8th lunar month called Chuseok. Both of these holidays occur in autumn, and Americans and Koreans eat special dishes comprised of local produce with their family members. However, despite these similarities, differences in the origin, focus, and traditional activities make Thanksgiving and Chuseok very distinct holidays.

While both Thanksgiving and Chuseok are holidays that date back several centuries, their origins are very different from each other. Previous to European explorers and colonists encountering the North American continent, many Europeans and Native Americans had autumn harvest festivals. Evidence suggests that Spanish explorers held a special holiday as early as the mid-sixteenth century, but the current holiday's origin is traced back to British settlers in Plymouth, celebrating a particularly good harvest in 1621 (Smith 4). On the other hand, Chuseok is a more ancient holiday originating in the Shilla Dynasty. It probably began as a celebration after a weaving competition, but it may have also been part of a celebration held after an important win over the Balhae Kingdom. Only later did this festival take on a stronger agricultural meaning related to the harvest and new moon. Therefore, while both Thanksgiving and Chuseok are very old festivals, they have very different origins and histories.

In addition to a harvest festival, today, both Americans and Koreans give thanks and show gratitude during their special holidays, but the focus of these feelings is different. Because Americans usually gather with their family members during the holiday, they often spend time reflecting on the importance of family and community. However, the present-day Thanksgiving holiday has also expanded to being thankful for many other parts of life, including health, employment, and new opportunities. In contrast, because of strong Shaman and Confucian traditions in Korea, Chuseok has become not only a time to spend with living family members, but also a time to honor and reflect on ancestors. Thus, while Americans reflect on the first Thanksgiving celebrations, most of their attention is on the present and their current blessings. In contrast, Koreans are more concerned with honoring the ancestors who made this life possible.

Finally, the differences between the origin and focus of Thanksgiving and Chuseok mean that the activities that Americans and Koreans participate in during their holidays are also different, with the exception of meeting with family members and eating elaborate meals. In the United States, students often participate in plays idealizing early Thanksgiving celebrations between Native Americans and Europeans. In addition, on the actual holiday, families watch parades or football games together in an effort to spend time with their loved ones. However, because honoring the dead is an important part of Chuseok, many Koreans participate in *charye*, which is an ancestral memorial ritual. Koreans also visit family burial plots to clean graves. After these duties are completed, they may watch archery or Korean wrestling competitions called *ssireum*, which date back to the Shilla Dynasty. In this way, both Americans and Koreans spend the holiday with their family members, but their activities reflect their different cultures.

Thanksgiving and Chuseok are often anticipated holidays because Americans and Koreans can spend time with their families while enjoying good seasonal food. However, despite these similarities, and the fact that Chuseok is often translated into English as “Korean Thanksgiving,” the two holidays have many differences. The different origins and focuses of these festivals have impacted the kinds of activities that have become customary. These differences which make the holidays unique festivals that both Americans and Koreans should learn about to understand the distinctiveness of American and Korean culture.

Activity 2

Answer the following questions about the essay you have just read.

1. Does this essay focus more on the similarities or the differences between the two holidays?
2. Make a list of the similarities and differences between two other holidays.

Structure

There are three basic structures found in compare and contrast writing: focus on the similarities, focus on the difference, and focus on the similarities and differences. The following structural examples are based on comparing and contrasting North American and Korean Christmas.

Focus on the Similarities

Paragraph	Topic	Korean and North American Information
Body Paragraph 1	Food	Eaten with loved ones, special dessert
Body Paragraph 2	Symbols	Christmas tree, red and green, lights
Body Paragraph 3	Santa Myth	Santa – large man who wears red, beard, delivers gifts

Focus on the Differences

Paragraph	Topic	Korean Information	North American Information
Body Paragraph 1	Food	Who: eaten with romantic partner or friends at a restaurant What: pizza, steak, wine, purchased Christmas cake	Who: eaten with family at home What: homemade turkey, ham, or goose, Christmas cookies, traditional dried fruit cake
Body Paragraph 2	Decorations	Mostly public: shopping areas, major streets, city areas Home: perhaps a small tree	Equally public and private: elaborate indoor and outdoor displays in homes, businesses, and public places
Body Paragraph 3	Santa Myth	1 reindeer (Rudolph), unknown home, family, and life	Several (perhaps 9) reindeer, Santa lives at the North Pole with his wife (Mrs. Claus) and elves (who make the toys)

Focus on the Similarities and Differences

Paragraph	Topic	Similarities	Differences
Body Paragraph 1	Food	Eaten with loved ones, special desserts	Korea: romantic partner/friends at restaurant eating pizza, steak, wine North America: family at home, homemade turkey, ham, or goose, Christmas cookies, traditional fruit cake
Body Paragraph 2	Decorations	Christmas tree, red and green, lights	Korea: mostly public, perhaps a small tree at home North America: elaborate indoor and outdoor displays in homes, businesses, and public areas
Body Paragraph 3	Santa Myth	Santa – large man who wears red, beard, delivers gifts	Korea: 1 reindeer, Santa's life unknown North America: 9 reindeer, North Pole, wife, helpers

Topic Selection

When choosing your topics for a compare and contrast assignment, you need to make sure that the topics are neither too similar nor too different. For instance, hamburgers and cheeseburgers are too similar to each other with the exception of a slice of cheese. In contrast, while ice cream and Siberia are both cold, the similarities end there. While deciding what you are going to write about, you should find two topics that are part of the same category with enough differences to make your paper interesting.

Activity 3

Look at the following topics and mark if they are too similar (S), too different (D), or good topics for a compare and contrast essay (G).

1. *Kimbab* vs. sandwiches
2. Japan vs. Japan Airlines (JAL)
3. Scuba diving vs. space walking
4. Caffe latte vs. americano
5. Action movie vs. Korean drama
6. Seollal vs. Solar New Year's Day
7. Turtles vs. snails
8. *Gochujang* vs. *jjimjilbang*
9. Seoul vs. Gyeongju
10. Vampires vs. witches

Venn Diagram Brainstorming

There are two ways to brainstorm for compare and contrast assignments. The first way is a Venn diagram, which is a visual way to show the similarities and differences between two topics. The following Venn Diagram shows the similarities and differences between Thanksgiving in the United States and Chuseok in South Korea.

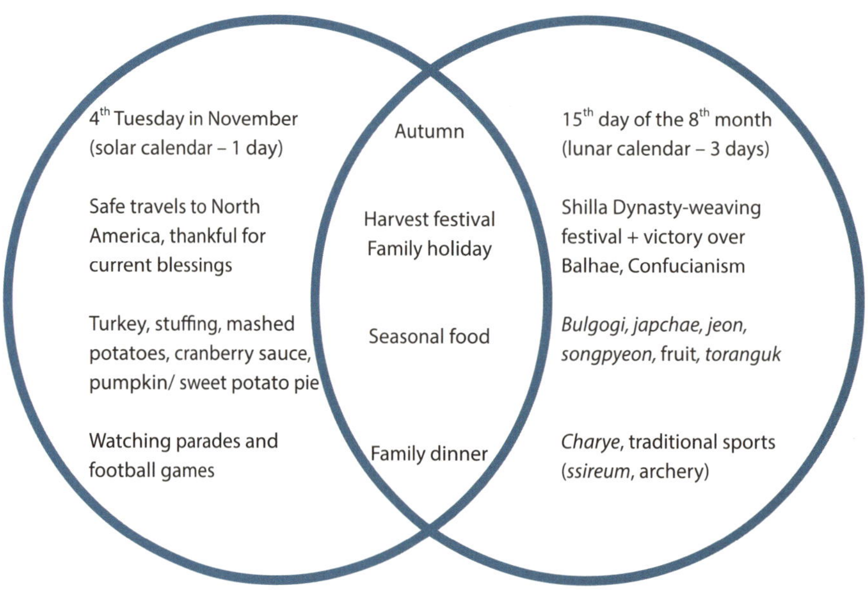

T-Chart Brainstorming

The second way to brainstorm for a compare and contrast assignment is a T-chart. This method works better for longer and more complicated assignments because there is more space available to develop each point. In this type of brainstorming, write the category on the left side and brainstorm the similarities and differences for each topic in the other columns. To differentiate between similarities and differences, use different colors of highlighters or underline the points that are different.

Category	The United States: Thanksgiving	Korea: Chuseok
When	• 4th Thursday in November • Solar calendar • Public holiday: One day	• 15th day of the 8th month • Lunar calendar • Public holiday: Three-five days
Origin	• Spanish 16th century/British 17th century • European and Native American harvest festivals • Good harvest/safe travels to North America	• Shilla Dynasty • A feast after a weaving contest • Victory over Balhae kingdom
Current Focus	• Family holiday • Harvest festival • Being thankful for present blessings	• Family holiday • Harvest festival • Ancestral memorial rituals
Food	• Turkey • Stuffing, mashed potatoes, sweet potatoes, squash • Pumpkin or sweet potato pie	• *Bulgogi* • *Japchae, jeon, toranguk* • *Songpyeon*, fruit
Activities	• Family dinner • Parades • Football games	• Family dinner • *Charye* and cleaning ancestors' graves • Traditional sports: *ssireum*, archery, tug of war

Compare and Contrast Connecting Words

Throughout your compare and contrast assignment, you should use connecting words to connect ideas and to make smooth transitions between different sections. The following are examples of both types of words.

Compare (Similarities)

likewise	similarly	furthermore	in addition	additionally
as	in the same way	also	too	moreover

Contrast (Differences)

yet	however	alternatively	conversely	although
in contrast	on the other hand	on the contrary	but	nevertheless

Activity 4

Take one of the good topic combinations in Activity 3, and brainstorm the similarities and differences in your notebook using a Venn diagram.

Activity 5

Use the ideas you brainstormed in Activity 4, and link them with connecting words to make full sentences.

Signpost See pages 16-19 for more information on connecting words. Some of the connecting words given above are coordinating conjunctions while others are subordinating conjunction words or transitions. Make sure you understand the differences between these kinds of words before you make your own sentences.

Activity 6

Use the sentences you made in Activity 5 to write a well-organized paragraph by adding a topic sentence and concluding sentence.

5 Cause and Effect Writing

Cause and effect writing shows the relationship between one idea or event and another, and thus it is a common style found in academic assignments, essays, and reports.

In business classes, students may be required to examine the negative effects of high staff turnover, or describe the reasons for low product sales. Engineering students may need to investigate the failings of a weight-bearing structure in a collapsed building or the effects of soil erosion. Students of history will often be asked to examine the causes and effects of historical events.

Cause and effect writing is favored by many teachers and professors because it requires the students to demonstrate critical thinking skills and analyze how events are related and connected to each other.

In this section you will:

- Examine a model cause and effect essay
- Analyze the different methods and organizational patterns of cause and effect writing
- Examine how cause and effect connectors are used to show a relationship
- Write a cause and effect essay

Activity 1

Answer the following questions about Cheonggyecheon.

1. Have you ever visited Cheonggyecheon? What are Cheonggyecheon's features?
2. What do you think are some of the advantages or disadvantages of having a stream or river flowing through the center of a city?

The Restoration of Cheonggyecheon

On July 1st, 2003, an ambitious plan led by the then mayor of Seoul, Lee, Myung Bak, began to restore the historic 600-year-old Cheonggyecheon stream that had been covered by road and expressway for over 30 years. The project was to take over two years and cost over 350 billion won, and it would eventually transform and revitalize the old central business district in Gangbuk, Seoul. When completed on September 30th 2005, a 5.86 kilometer long stream and green pathway were unveiled that would become one of the most popular tourist attractions in Seoul. Dr. K.Y. Hwang described Cheonggyecheon as a symbol of the transformation of Seoul into a world class city (89). There have been a number of positive effects resulting from the restoration of Cheonggycheon, with the project becoming a vehicle for environmental change, economic revitalization, and cultural renaissance.

One of the most noticeable and immediate effects of the Cheonggyecheon restoration project was the improvement in environmental quality in the Gangbuk central business district (CBD). As a result of the removal of the elevated highway that stood above the historic waterway and the reorganization of the public transport system, a dramatic reduction in the amount of traffic entering downtown ensued. Consequently, air quality improved drastically. In addition to a decrease in air pollution, the reduction of vehicles helped to reduce the temperature in the downtown area. The removal of the existing elevated highway, in conjunction with the flow of water and air down the stream, resulted in a reduction in temperature in the CBD of around 10-13% (91). Environmental quality has also been enhanced by the creation of new natural habitats along the stream, thus many bird and insect species have returned. In addition, the introduction of various species of fish into the stream has also contributed to the re-establishment of Cheonggyecheon as a living space. As a consequence of the enhancement of atmospheric quality and the construction of green spaces, a new ecologically friendly environment has been created for citizens to enjoy.

In addition to the environmental transformation, the restoration of Cheonggyecheon has also helped to revitalize the CBD and stimulate economic development. During the last few decades, Seoul city has focused its efforts on developing the Gangnam area; as a consequence, the old CBD located in Gangbuk had contracted (85). One of the main objectives of the Cheonggyecheon restoration project was to initiate a balanced development between north and south Seoul, and the revitalization of the Cheonggyecheon area helped this considerably. The Cheonggyecheon project has been a catalyst for urban expansion and commercial success in the area resulting in the return of both international and national regional headquarters to the Gangbuk area around the Cheonggyecheon. For example, in early 2011 the 80 billion won Mirae Assets Center One Building was opened alongside the historic stream. There can be no doubt that the vitality of the Gangbuk CBD has been greatly enhanced by the restoration of Cheonggyecheon.

Finally, the restoration of Cheonggyecheon has resulted in the re-establishment of the culture and historical heritage in and around the Gangbuk area. According to Kim, Nam Joon, a professor in the Department of Landscape Architecture at Dankook University, "The restoration project of Cheonggyecheon is, not only a part of Seoul's urban planning, but a symbolic project to revive an important part of Korea's historical and natural heritage at the start of the twenty-first century" (81). Due to the restoration of historical objects like Gwangtonggyo Bridge, many of the cultural treasures hidden from the citizens of Seoul for decades have been uncovered again. To create a synergy between culture and tourism, the Seoul Foundation for the Arts and Culture has initiated a number of festivals, including the Cheonggyecheon Art Festival and the Seoul Lantern Festival, both held in the Cheonggyecheon area. As a consequence, the Gangbuk CBD is regaining its position in Seoul as the place to be. For over six centuries, Cheonggyecheon itself was a part of the culture and heritage of Seoul. Now, after three decades of being buried, it is once again in the spotlight and has led to a cultural renaissance in Seoul.

Since its re-opening in September 2005, Cheonggyecheon has become a beneficial feature in the lives of Seoulites. The restoration of the historic waterway has helped to invigorate the local environment through the creation of a cooler, healthier CBD, and the re-creation of natural habitats has resulted in life returning to an area that had been choking on automobile exhaust for almost 30 years. Economic balance in Seoul has been restored as investors have returned to the old CBD, thus the local economy has been revitalized. Most importantly, perhaps, Cheonggyecheon has provided a cultural green space and events venue for both Korean citizens and overseas tourists to enjoy. There is no doubt that Cheonggyecheon is once again an important asset to the citizens of Seoul. In the future it will continue to be loved and enjoyed by the people who use it, making it the veritable soul of the city.

Activity 2

Answer the following questions about the essay.

1. Does this essay state the effects from the restoration of Cheonggyecheon, the causes for the restoration of Cheonggyecheon, or both?

2. What are the three main effects of the restoration of Cheonggyecheon? For each body idea, find three supporting examples stated in the essay.

B1 ____________________

B2 ____________________

B3 ____________________

3. In your town or city, choose a historic, famous, or interesting place, and write down any effects it may have on the citizens and the town/city itself.

Organization of a Cause-Effect Essay

Once a topic has been given or chosen, the way the essay will be organized should be decided. A writer may wish to examine the causes, effects, or both.

Focus on Causes Method

Using this method, the writer will discuss the causes for an event or condition and develop and discuss each cause in each body paragraph. In the following example, the writer will discuss the factors that can cause heart disease to increase.

Cause	Effect
A person has a poor diet	The risk of heart disease increases
A person smokes	
A person has a family history of high blood pressure	

Focus on Effects Method

Using this method, the writer will discuss the effects of an event or condition and develop and discuss each effect in each body paragraph. In the following example, the writer will discuss the effects resulting from a poor diet.

Cause	Effect
People have a poor diet.	They may gain weight
	They may suffer from fatigue
	They may develop non-insulin diabetes

Activity 3

Fill in the tables with appropriate information to complete the cause-effect relationship.

Cause	Effect
Ji Su goes to the library everyday.	
Ji Su studies hard on the weekends.	
Ji Su takes extra classes.	

Cause	Effect
A country hosts the Olympic Games.	

Focus on Causes and Effects Method (Chain Organization)

Using this method, the writer will discuss the both the causes and effects of an event or condition. The effect from the previous paragraph will then become the cause in the preceding paragraph. The causes and effects are therefore linked like a chain with each having an influence on the next. In the following example, the writer will discuss the links leading from a poor diet to an increase in the risk of heart disease.

How diet affects health

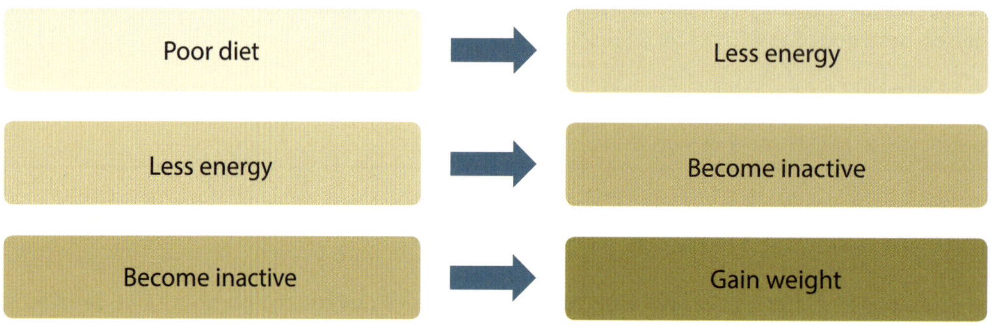

Getting a part time job

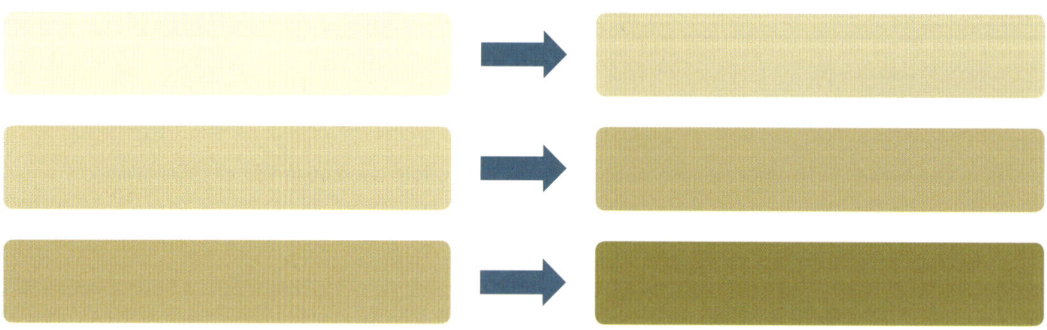

Signpost When developing ideas in a chain organization, the writer needs to be careful to avoid logical fallacies. See page 164.

Cause-Effect Organization

When developing the causes or effects in an essay, you can organize the body in two ways: order of importance and chronological (time) order.

1. Order of importance: This format is where ideas are arranged from the weakest to the strongest. In the essay on the restoration of Cheonggyecheon, the writer believes that the re-establishment of the cultural and historical heritage is the most important factor. A different writer, such as an economics or business major, may feel that the stimulation of the local economy is the most important and thereby the final effect to discuss.
2. Chronological order: This format is where ideas are arranged into a time order from what happened first to last. Cause-effect writing dealing with history is often arranged chronologically.

Cause-Effect Connecting Words

Just as connecting words are used in other types of writing, so too are they used to show or express the relationship between ideas.

Cause

Because Since As	the costs were high,	the project was cancelled
As a result of As a consequence of Because of Due to	the high costs	

Effect

The costs were too high;	as a result, as a consequence, thus, therefore, consequently, hence,	the project was cancelled

Activity 4

In the model essay, a number of connectors have been used to show the cause/effect relationship. Go back through the essay and highlight any cause/effect connectors.

Activity 5

Choose one of the three following topics, and create the body outline for an essay. What method of organization will you use?

The growth of Seoul	The high divorce rate	Increased life expectancy

1. Body Paragraph 1: ______________________
   a. Supporting detail 1: ______________________
   ____
   b. Supporting detail 2: ______________________
   ____
   c. Supporting detail 3: ______________________
   ____
2. Body Paragraph 2: ______________________
   a. Supporting detail 1: ______________________
   ____
   b. Supporting detail 2: ______________________
   ____
   c. Supporting detail 3: ______________________
   ____
3. Body Paragraph 3: ______________________
   a. Supporting detail 1: ______________________
   ____
   b. Supporting detail 2: ______________________
   ____
   c. Supporting detail 3: ______________________
   ____

Activity 6

Using what you have learned so far, write a cause and effect essay.

6 Persuasive Writing

Persuasive writing is writing in which writers give their opinion and the reasons for their opinion with the aim of convincing the reader to agree with them. The writer appeals to logic and evidence in order to make a strong case for their argument and addresses the questions or objections the reader may have. Good persuasive writing should include sufficient evidence, and this requires research on the part of the writer.

We are constantly exposed to persuasion through the media and through interactions with our friends. We are persuaded to buy products, watch shows and films, listen to music, read publications, and of course, believe certain opinions. Persuasive writing is one method of presenting a convincing message or argument to an audience of readers. You might want to persuade a prospective employer to invite you for an interview, or maybe you want to persuade people to avoid using a particular telephone service after your own bad experience. Maybe you are passionate about a current issue, and you wish to convince others to think in the same way.

Persuasive strategies also increase your awareness of the subtle as well as not-so-subtle ways in which you are targeted for persuasion each day. Understanding these strategies can help us to make better decisions in the future.

In this section you will:

- Examine a model persuasive paragraph and essay
- Learn about the components of persuasive writing
- Analyze the structure of a persuasive paragraph and essay
- Learn to identify and use persuasive techniques
- Write a persuasive paragraph and essay

Activity 1

Answer the following questions about academic life.

1. What are the advantages and disadvantages of taking a year off between high school and university?
2. Do you plan to take any time off before you graduate? If so, what will you do? If not, why not?

Persuasive Paragraph

Benefits of a Year Off

Many students are ill-prepared to make the transition from high school to university. Therefore, students should take a year off between high school and university. First of all, most students have known only academic life since their childhood. By the end of their 12 years of schooling, students are often tired of the routine. Time off provides a break from study in which young people can explore other interests before returning to academia to start their university career with renewed vigor and greater maturity. This time is also an opportunity to travel, which increases independence. This is very important for university life, where students are expected to take responsibility for their own learning. Finally, taking a year off gives students a chance to work. This can add valuable experience to the résumé as well as helping financially equip students for an increasingly expensive university education. In conclusion, a year off is a chance for young people to recharge, grow in independence and maturity, and gain valuable experience and cash to prepare them for college life and beyond.

Persuasive Essay

Benefits of a Year Off

Most Korean students expect to finish high school with the trauma of the Korean Scholastic Aptitude Test (KSAT). The intense stress of the exam and the pressure of the preceding years of study leave many students ill-prepared to embark on university life. The obvious solution is to take a year off between high school and university, and an increasing number of universities have formal policies that allow students to take a year off of study by deferring their placement. However, some argue that this is a waste of time and students are better off focusing on their education. While there is some logic to this argument, the potential benefits of a year off make it time well spent. Although this time off delays graduation and the start of a career, students should take a year out between school and university for their mental health, rich experiences, and the augmentation of their résumé.

First, by taking a year off students can recover from the long and arduous education marathon. By the time they finish high school, the average student will have spent around 15,000 hours in school: almost two full years, day and night. Most students have known nothing but the term/vacation cycle since starting school at the age of five. The final leg of this epic academic journey is the Korean Scholastic Aptitude Test (KSAT) which is seen as the most important exam that Korean students will ever face since it decides the students' fate in higher education. They are under great pressure to achieve a high ranking in order to attend a reputable university and gain the advantages of an elite education. This intensity can lead to what J. Lee et al. identify as "academic burnout" (16). Taking a year off is a way for students to take a thorough break from academia and recuperate from the stresses of the KSAT. This will, therefore, make them mentally better equipped to start their university studies with fresh enthusiasm for learning.

Not only is a year off a good opportunity to recuperate and reflect, but it is also a unique chance for young people to gain valuable life experience. One popular and rewarding way to spend a year off is to travel. It has long been popular for students to spend up to a year exploring the world before entering university. Since the 1960s, students have been taking advantage of time away from school to experience new cultures, learn languages, and gain valuable life experiences. Many universities regard a year off very highly and there are organizations that help students make the most of their time through volunteer work and language programs in order to give them valuable skills and experiences to further appeal to top colleges and even employers. Thus, travel can be a good way to gain understanding of the world and develop skills that appeal to universities and employers.

For some, travel may be too expensive an option, but a year off can be a good chance to earn money, gain work experience, and develop valuable life skills. Another advantage of taking time away from school is that it is a chance to get a full-time job. According to the Korean Education Ministry, public university fees increased from 2.9 to 4.19 million won, or 44.5% between 2004 and 2009 (16). The report also shows that private university fees increased from 5.77 million won to 7.42 million won, or 28% over the same period. A year off gives students a chance to earn money to pay for some of these costs and reduce the burden on their family. An additional benefit is the opportunity to gain valuable experience and make useful contacts which are increasingly important in today's competitive job market. Finally, a year of working with adults is a good way for young people to learn about the expectations and realities of the adult world. Therefore, the experience helps them to mature and set realistic goals based on their knowledge of real-life.

In conclusion, high school graduates should take a year off before starting university in order to revive their enthusiasm for study, see the world, and improve their résumé. Some disagree, suggesting that the year would be better spent as a freshman student. However, many students suffer from academic burnout and benefit greatly from a year off. There are many advantages to taking time to see the world when one is young and free from responsibilities that come after graduation. Furthermore, a year off can be well spent working to earn money for tuition fees and gaining experience in a relevant field. Students taking a year off are better prepared for a successful future.

Activity 2

Answer the following questions about the essay.

1. In your own words, what is the writer's opinion?

____

____

2. What were the three reasons for his or her opinion?

____

____

3. What do you think is the strongest reason? Why?

____

____

4. Do you agree with the writer's opinion? Why or why not?

____

____

Fact vs. Opinion

In persuasive writing, writers usually present an opinion and then use a variety of strategies to convince the reader that the opinion is reasonable. Therefore, writers must understand the difference between fact and opinion. A fact is a verifiable truth or certainty: "The actor Christopher Lee played Count Dracula in nine different films." An opinion is a personal thought or position: "Christopher Lee was the best Count Dracula."

It is important to remember that the wording of facts and opinions is very important. For example, "Roger Moore is my favorite James Bond" is actually a fact about an opinion. In the same way, "My grandfather hates dentists" is a fact about my grandfather's opinion of dentists.

Activity 3

Read the following sentences, and identify which are facts (F) and which are opinions (O).

1. Lee, Sun Shin was born in Hanseong (now Seoul) in 1545. ______
2. The woolly rhinoceros lived in Asia and Europe until around 10,000 years ago. ______
3. Steve Jobs was the most important person of his generation. ______
4. In Shi'a culture, couples occasionally enter into temporary marriages in which they agree to a term of commitment from between one hour and 99 years. ______
5. Temporary marriage should be introduced into every culture. ______
6. Space colonies are the only way to prevent the extinction of our species. ______
7. Since more people are killed in horse racing than any other sport, horse racing should be banned. ______
8. The number of Internet users in China increased from 22 million to 450 million between 2000 and 2010. ______
9. Climate change is the biggest global issue these days. ______
10. My teacher thinks that students should take a year to work or travel after finishing high school and before starting university. ______

Persuasive Paragraph Structure

The persuasive paragraph follows the same structure as any other paragraph. It usually starts with an introductory sentence to give background information. It then has a topic sentence, which gives the writer's opinion. The body of the paragraph usually gives three reasons for the opinion. Finally, there is the conclusion in which the writer restates his or her opinion.

Introduction sentence: Give some brief background to your topic so the reader can understand your opinion.

Topic sentence: Write a sentence that gives your opinion in a clear, concise way.

Reason 1: What is the first reason for your opinion? How can you back this up?

Reason 2: Give the second reason for your opinion.

Reason 3: Give the third reason for your opinion.

Concluding sentence: Restate your opinion in different words.

Signpost See page 47 for more information on paragraph outlines.

Activity 4

Read the example persuasive paragraph on page 118 and complete the outline.

Topic: Year Off

Topic sentence: ______________________

Reason 1: ______________________

Reason 2: ______________________

Reason 3: ______________________

Concluding sentence: ______________________

Topic

When choosing a topic for a persuasive writing assignment, it is very important to consider two questions:

1. What are you interested in? You will probably write a better essay if you write on a topic you are passionate about.
2. What is the purpose of your writing? If you are writing an assignment, your teacher will probably give you some guidelines, such as a topic area or an imaginary audience. Think about what your teacher wants you to show them through your writing and select a topic that will help you to meet these goals. If you are writing for another purpose, think about your intended audience. Use appropriate language and terminology, and pick examples that will appeal to them.

Activity 5

Write a question for each of the following topics. Then answer one question and give three reasons for your answer.

Topic: Pets

Question: Should people in one room apartments keep pets?

Opinion (Thesis): People in small apartments should keep pets.

1. Pets are great companions. People in one room apartments are probably single and lonely.
2. Pets are entertaining. People can have more fun with a pet than watching television.
3. Small houses are good places for small pets, such as hamsters.

Plastic Surgery	Nuclear Power	The Death Penalty	Euthanasia

Topic: ______________________________

Question: ______________________________

Opinion: ______________________________

Reason 1: ______________________________

Reason 2: ______________________________

Reason 3: ______________________________

Persuasive Essay Structure

A five-paragraph persuasive essay contains the basic essay components: Introductory paragraph, body paragraphs, and concluding paragraph. The writer's opinion is given in the thesis statement, and it is supported with facts and evidence in the body paragraphs. The restated thesis in the conclusion gives the opinion one more time, along with a summary of the reasons.

Introductory paragraph: Include a hook, relevant background information, and finish with the thesis statement and opinion.

Body paragraphs: Give the reasons for your opinion. Back them up with evidence.

Concluding paragraph: Restate your opinion and give a strong summary of your reasons. Finish with a clear wrap-up sentence.

A good persuasive essay should:

- Begin with an appropriate hook
- Phrase the opinion as a strong statement
- Include qualifiers (e.g. most instead of all, usually instead of always)
- Include reasons that appeal to the intended reader
- Use facts to support the argument
- Give credible sources for supporting information
- Be logical and internally consistent
- Include a counterargument: Acknowledge the opposing viewpoint and refute it
- Restate the opinion in the conclusion
- Conclude memorably and have a clear wrap-up sentence

Seeing Both Sides

When writing a persuasive piece, good writers consider opposing opinions in order to present a more reasonable argument. It allows the writer to explain why opposing viewpoints are less reasonable than the one being argued for.

Activity 6

Choose one of the following opinions and write a list of ideas for and against it.

1. All captive animals should be released into the wild.
2. Young people should have plastic surgery to improve their appearance.
3. All university lectures should be broadcast online instead of being taught live in class.
4. Children should be homeschooled.
5. The subway is better than the bus.

For	Against

Counterarguments

A counterargument is an opposing viewpoint the writer uses to address the concerns or doubts of the reader and then refutes them with sound reasoning. The advantages of including a counterargument in your persuasive writing are:

1. It shows that you have considered opposing viewpoints and opinions.
2. It directly confronts possible objections the reader may have.
3. It shows that you are a considerate writer and therefore makes your opinion more compelling.

There are four steps to writing a counterargument:

Step 1: Identify an opposing viewpoint.

Some people argue that homeschooling isolates children from their peers.

Objection phrases

One might object...
A possible objection might be...
Some people argue that...

Step 2: Comment on the validity or strength of this viewpoint.

It is true that homeschooled children interact with fewer children during the day, but...

Concession phrases

It is true that..., but...
While this is sometimes true...
This may be true in some cases...
This is rarely true...
It has never been shown to be the case...
It is not actually the case that...

Step 3: Provide your point of view (refutation).

Refutation phrases

However, ...
It is also true that...
Studies show that...
This is not applicable because...

Step 4: Provide a strong reason or evidence to support your opinion over the opposing opinion.

... homeschooling is often done with groups of children from several families. Studies show that they form stronger relationships than children who interact in the more populous school environment. Furthermore, there are plenty of opportunities for outside activities in the community, including sports teams and clubs.

Activity 7

Write a counterargument for the following opinion.

People who do military service should not have to pay university tuition fees.

Opposing viewpoint: ______________________________

Concession: ______________________________

Refutation: ______________________________

Support: ______________________________

Wrap-up Sentence

The final sentence in the essay can be used to make a final comment about your topic or opinion. However, in a persuasive essay, it is sometimes necessary to finish with a "call to action."

For example, for the topic "The benefits of flossing," the action would be to buy some dental floss and floss each day after meals. If your essay is persuasive enough, the reader is likely to do it.

Signpost See page 80 for more information on concluding memorably.

Activity 8

Write some actions to match the following topics.

Topic	Action
The AIDS epidemic	______________
Abandoned animals	______________
Vivisection (Animal testing)	______________
The disabled	______________
The environment	______________

Activity 9

Write a persuasive essay.

Building Blocks

The basic foundation for all writing is the sentence. Grammatically sound sentences help writers to convey their message properly and accurately, but beyond grammar, there are also skills and techniques students can learn in order to enhance their writing and clarify their points. This section will help students to review basic grammar before moving into more complex skills and techniques students can use to improve their ability to write academically and objectively. A great deal of space is available for students to practice and perfect these skills before they try to bring them into longer paragraph and essay assignments.

This section does not have to be followed in a linear way. Rather, the information covered in these subsections can be incorporated into various forms of writing and contexts. The main point of this section is to help students develop the skills necessary to enrich their sentences and improve their overall writing techniques.

This section covers:

- Articles
- Capitalization
- Prepositions
- Conditionals
- Modals
- Adjectives
- Active vs. Passive Voice
- Comparatives and Superlatives
- Using Non-English Words in English
- Academic Writing Techniques
- Logical Fallacies
- Paraphrasing and Summarizing

1 Articles

"A" and "an" are indefinite articles used to identify general nouns while "the" is the definite article which is used to refer to specific nouns.

Examples:

Neils Bohr was **a** Danish physicist. (one of many Danish physicists)

Neils Bohr was **the** physicist who first drew the structure of the atom. (the first to do something)

The students found **an** empty classroom, so they could study. (any room is fine)

The students could not find **the** classroom for their English class. (the specific room)

Indefinite Articles

"A" is used with words that sound like consonants while "an" is used with words that sound like vowels. In some words, vowels sound like consonants, so they need an "a" while in some words, consonants sound like vowels and should be preceded by an "an."

Examples:

When she was **a** sophomore, Jeong Ah only spent **an** hour on **an** eight page essay about **a** United Nations agency, so her professor gave her **an** "F."

Countable and Uncountable Nouns

"A" and "an" can only be used with countable nouns.

Countable	Uncountable	Both
Pear	Rice	Do you want **a chocolate**? (individual piece) I do not like **chocolate**. (in general)
Dollar	Money	He does not have **a hair** on his head. (individual strand) She just dyed her **hair** red. (whole head of hair)
Horse	Love	Is there **an extra room** in International Hall? (classroom) Do you have **room** in your car for me? (space)
Pen	Information	Is there **a light** in each room? (light fixture) Our new house has more **light**. (natural light)
Table	Equipment	**A scary experience** happened today. (occurrence) I have enough **experience** for this job. (general)

Examples:

If you have a pen, I will write down information about equipment you can buy to make homemade chocolate.

Definite Articles

Like many areas of English grammar, there are some exceptions in how definite articles are used. Nevertheless, "the" is usually used in the following situations:

Use	Examples
Something previously mentioned	There is an unoccupied chair, but the chair looks broken.
Something specific or unique	The professor for this class just arrived.
A group of people identified by an adjective or a population as a whole	the unemployed, the Spanish
Instruments	the piano
Superlatives	the fastest
Plural names of groups of people and places	the Kims, the Netherlands
Country names including 'republic' and 'united'	the Republic of Ireland, the United Kingdom
Buildings (unless the first word is the name of a place)	the Blue House
Oceans, seas, rivers, canals, gulfs, peninsulas, gulfs, deserts	the Pacific Ocean, the Black Sea, the Amazon, the Panama Canal
Mountain, island, or lake groups	the Himalayas, the Canary Islands, the Connecticut Lakes
Geographical regions, points on the globe, location	the West, the Equator, Gwangju is in the southern part of Korea.

Do not use "the" in the following situations:

Use	Examples
Most languages, nationalities	English, Australian
Continents, most countries, states/provinces	Europe, Morocco, British Columbia
Buildings (if the first word is the name of a place)	Seoul Liberty Building
Cities/towns, streets	Incheon, Main Street
Bays, parks, individual mountains, islands, or lakes	James Bay, Hyde Park, Bukhan Mountain, Easter Island, Lake Louise
Directions (when comparing two places)	Nepal is north of India.

Grammar Tip Using Non-English Words

Non-English words usually follow the same countable/non countable rules.

Activity 1

Correct the articles in the following sentences.

1. Before going on a hike, remember to pack a water, the chocolate bars, and map.
2. Young children should learn the Korean before they learn second language.
3. At the pet shop beside the Summer Hill Park, there were a snakes, a iguana, and the turtle.
4. The Seoul is located on Korean Peninsula in South Korea, which is also called Republic of Korea.
5. Renee will not eat chicken because she has chicken for the pet.
6. Jenny had always wanted to work in the large company, but a company she wanted to work in would not hire her, so she joined small company instead.
7. White House is official residence for President of United States.
8. Homeless in Seoul often find shelter in a Seoul Station on cold nights.
9. Kennedys live on the St. Denis street which is located the north of St. Laurent street.
10. Chinese in the Taiwan speak Mandarin, and Chinese in Guangdong province speak Cantonese.
11. He wants to eat *kimchi*; however, *kimchi* in his refrigerator is now rotten.
12. June does not like the *ddeok*, but she ate piece of *ddeok* because it was served at her friend's wedding.
13. I would give you piece of paper, but there is no the paper left.

Activity 2

After reading the following passages, fill in the missing articles.

Yeon Hee has violin that costs over million dollars because she is professional violinist. She has been playing violin since she was three years old, and she won first prize in her second competition when she was only four. At age seven, she was accepted into prestigious Seoul Performing Arts Academy and quickly progressed to senior position in youth orchestra. Later, Yeon Hee moved to the London when she was 15 years old to pursue her dream of becoming professional violinist. These days Yeon Hee regularly plays with London Symphony Orchestra, but she has yet to be asked to be soloist.

Great Lakes are five lakes located along Canadian-American border. While each lake is a separate body of water, they are connected through rivers and canals. For instance, Niagara River connects Lake Huron to Lake Ontario at the city of Niagara Falls, and Welland Canal connects Lake Erie and Lake Ontario. Saint Lawrence River takes the water from all of these lakes to Atlantic Ocean by way of Quebec and Gaspé Peninsula. Water in these lakes provides water and power to many important North American cities surrounding lakes including Chicago, Detroit, and Toronto.

2 Capitalization

When English letters are written in their uppercase form, the process is called "capitalization." The following chart shows when letters are usually capitalized.

Use	Examples
The first word of a sentence	Exchange programs provide students with many benefits.
"I"	When I was in high school, I studied until midnight every night.
Every word in a title (except articles, prepositions, and coordinating conjunctions unless they appear at the beginning of a title)	*The Wind in the Willows*
Proper nouns (Specific or unique nouns)	
• Organizations	• the World Health Organization.
• Places	• Sungkyunkwan University is an old university.
• Brands	• Starbucks Coffee Company has good coffee.
• Geographical regions	• There are many conflicts in the Middle East.
• Names, titles, names before titles, titles before names	• Professor Lee is a famous professor. • Aunt Sarah is my favorite aunt.
• Days, months, holidays	• In 2011, Children's Day, which is always on May 5th, fell on a Thursday.
Words derived from proper nouns (adjectives, languages, etc)	Spanish is spoken in Spain by Spaniards.
Course titles	Because he was a biology major, he took Introduction to Biology.

Grammar Tip Capitalization and Names

Some names have unique capitalization rules because of their origin.

Jane McNeil Osama bin Laden Vincent van Gogh

Korean names are generally capitalized in one of four ways.

Young Sang Lee Young-Sang Lee Youngsang Lee Lee, Youngsang

Whichever way you choose to capitalize Korean names, you should remain consistent in your writing.

Activity 1

Read the following sentences, and highlight the words which should be capitalized.

1. before i went to portugal last year, i studied portuguese.
2. sam failed history 101 last year because history is his worst subject.
3. professor lee asked john if he had finished reading jane austen's *pride and prejudice*.
4. there is a mr. pizza pizza restaurant located very close to hyehwa station.
5. when korean thanksgiving falls on a tuesday or thursday, it is a five day holiday, but when it falls on a saturday, sunday, or wednesday, it is only a three day holiday.
6. there are many ways to experience nature in seoul: bukhan mountain, the han river, and cheonggye stream.
7. after watching the movie *the devil wears prada*, jenny decided to go to new york city instead of visiting europe.
8. there is about 1,050 mg of sodium in a serving of shin ramyun which is surprisingly more sodium than the 1,010 mg found in a mcdonald's big mac.
9. lee hyo ri's song "chitty chitty bang bang" has nothing to do with ian fleming's 1964 novel by the same name.
10. professor webster is a south african anthropologist who is best known for his contribution to the anti–apartheid movement.

Activity 2

Read the following passages and highlight the letters which should be capitalized.

shanghai, in the people's republic of china, is a fabulous city to visit. tourists who love sports can visit during the chinese grand prix or watch the city's basketball team, the shanghai sharks play. for those who prefer to spend their time in museums, the shanghai art museum in people's square houses a large number of exhibitions. at night, the bund is a fantastic area to see historic buildings and view architecturally interesting buildings such as the oriental pearl tower across the huangpu river. therefore, there are many diverse places to visit and sites to see in shanghai.

ban, ki moon has had an interesting life. he was born in a small village in north chungcheong province, but in 1962, he won a red cross essay contest which allowed him to move to san francisco where he was able to improve his english skills. during his time in the united states of america, he met president john f. kennedy. after attending seoul national university and harvard university, he became a diplomat and later, the head of the ministry of foreign affairs and trade in south korea. he presently holds the position of secretary general at the united nations. thus, his life is an inspiration for younger koreans who want to serve their country on an international level.

3 Prepositions

Prepositions of Time

The following prepositions are commonly used to discuss time.

Preposition	Use	Examples
At	Precise times	Class begins at 9 am. We take a break at dinnertime.
In	General times • months, years, centuries, long periods	He was born in July in 1980. Sungkyunkwan University was founded in the 14th century. We have class in the morning.
On	Specific times • dates and days	His birthday is on July 31. On White Day, men give women candy.
During	Development through a period	During the month of July, there is often a lot of rain. During the Seollal period, there are no classes.
For	Length of time	We have been in class for twenty minutes.
Since	Beginning of a period	We have been in class since 9 am.
Until	Continuance until a specific time	You will have until the end of class to finish the exam. Students have until December 1st to hand in their papers.
From-To	A specific time period	You will have from 9 am to 10:15 am to finish the exam.

Prepositions of Location

The following prepositions are often used to discuss the location of a person or object.

Preposition	Use	Examples
At	General spaces Paper Groups of people	At the bus stop, at the movie theater. At the top/bottom of the page At the front/back of the class
In	Spaces with boundaries Bodies of water Lines	I am watching a movie in the theater. In the sea In a row/in a line
On	Surfaces Small islands Directions	On the wall/table On Maui On the left/right

Grammar Tip Irregular Examples

Travel:	on foot	in taxis/cars	on bikes/boats/public transportation
Corner:	in a room corner	at/on a street corner	

Prepositions of Space

The following are common prepositions to explain where an object or a person is located.

Above	Around	Beyond	Near	Through
Across	Behind	By	Nearby	Toward
Against	Below	Down	Next to	Under
Ahead of	Beneath	From	On top of	Underneath
Along	Beside	In front of	Outside (of)	Up
Among	Between	Inside	Over	Within

Grammar Tip

Students need to also be aware of how prepositions are used with media.

The song was on the radio.
I saw a program on television.
I read the essay in a book/newspaper/magazine.
He listens to the radio every day.
I read the article on the Internet.

Activity 1

Complete the following sentences.

1. Are your children __________ the festival?
2. There is a beautiful picture __________ the wall.
3. I am __________ school, __________ the classroom, __________ the fourth floor.
4. ________ as long as I can remember, that elderly man has lived ____________ that house __________ the corner of the street.
5. I missed my favorite program __________ television because I was reading a very exciting part ___________ my book, so I had to watch the show later ___________ the Internet.

Activity 2

Read the following sentences and insert the appropriate prepositions where necessary.

1. Jane is arriving January 26th 2 o'clock the afternoon.
2. It snows here every year December, so we always go outside and play the snow Christmas Day.
3. Michael came here foot, but because of the flood, he had to leave a boat.
4. Frankie started working for her law firm 1995.
5. Jill began working on the project yesterday.
6. 2003, the students have eaten the cafeteria lunchtime. However, before there was a cafeteria, the students usually ate the large leafy trees.
7. When the taxis are a line, you have to take the taxi the others.
8. The students the back of the class should write their names the top of the page.
9. At the moment, he is Jeju Island, but because he is afraid of fish the water, he is spending all of his time his hotel swimming pool.
10. You have 10 am 11 am to complete the exam. Please write all of the information the box provided. Please also remember to keep your eyes the paper, and do not look at the papers of the students sitting you.
11. Over a year, a burglar has been breaking into buildings late night and stealing jewelry from locked cases. One night, a police officer heard a noise and went to investigate. The burglar heard him, so he jumped out of a window and into a truck. However, the police officer saw the numbers the license plate and was able to catch the criminal.

4 Conditionals

Conditionals are used to show cause and effect relationships. They are complex sentences which consist of an "if" (sometimes "when") subordinating clause and a "main" independent clause.

Type	Construction	Examples
Type 0 Usual, habitual, or scientific fact	**If/When**: present simple **Main**: present simple	When I come to school, I take the bus. If I drink tea, I drink green tea. When water reaches 71 degrees at the top of Mt. Everest, it boils.
Type 1 Possible, likely to happen in the near future	**If**: present simple **Main**: will + base verb	If the weather is warm, we will go swimming. If I have an "A" average, I will get a scholarship. If the situation continues, profits will decrease.
Type 2 Unreal, unlikely to happen in the present	**If**: past simple **Main**: would*** + base verb	If aliens attacked, I would fight them. If I were you, I would not do that. If I saw a burglary, I would call the police.
Type 3 Impossible past, regrets, imagining a different reality based on a different past	**If**: past perfect **Main**: would have + past participle	If aliens had attacked, I would have fought them. If I had been you, I would not have done that. If I had seen a burglary, I would have called the police.

***In Type 2 or 3 conditionals, "would" can be replaced with "might" (possibility) or "could" (option/ability).

Grammar Tip

In some cases, more than one type can be used to show different meanings.

Examples:
If I become the President, I will lower taxes. (a candidate in an election)
If I became the President, I would lower taxes. (regular people)

If our team wins, we will all cheer. (optimistic)
If our team won, we would all cheer. (pessimistic)

Grammar Tip Second Conditional

When using the second conditional in the first person, use "were" instead of "was."
Example: If I were you, I would apply for the position.

Activity 1

Identify the following conditionals, and answer the questions.

1. When you exercise, what kind of exercise do you do? Type: 0 / 1 / 2 / 3

When I exercise, I play basketball.

2. If you were a pig, how would your life be different? Type: 0 / 1 / 2 / 3

3. If there is yellow dust tomorrow, will you go hiking? Type: 0 / 1 / 2 / 3

4. If you moved to another country, where would you want to live? Type: 0 / 1 / 2 / 3

5. If you get a job this vacation, what kind of work will you do? Type: 0 / 1 / 2 / 3

6. When you feel sad, how do you make yourself feel happy again? Type: 0 / 1 / 2 / 3

7. If you meet your friends this weekend, where will you go? Type: 0 / 1 / 2 / 3

8. If you saw a murder being committed, what would you do? Type: 0 / 1 / 2 / 3

9. If North Korea had won the Korean War, how would life have been different?
Type: 0 / 1 / 2 / 3

10. If you had failed the college entrance exam ten times, what would you have done?
Type: 0 / 1 / 2 / 3

____

11. If you found a wallet filled with money on the street, what would you do with it?
Type: 0 / 1 / 2 / 3

____

12. When you have a cold, what do you do to get better? Type: 0 / 1 / 2 / 3

____

13. If you had been born 100 years ago, how would your life have been different?
Type: 0 / 1 / 2 / 3

____

14. If you saw your friend cheat on a test, what would you do? Type: 0 / 1 / 2 / 3

____

Activity 2

On a separate piece of paper, make your own Type 0–3 conditionals for another classmate to answer.

Activity 3

Choose one of the topics from Activity 1, and write a paragraph on the topic.

5 Modals

Modal verbs modify other verbs to show permission, ability, possibility, and obligation.

Permission/Request

Can	Informal – question	Can I have some water?
May	Formal – question	May I borrow your pen?
Could	Formal – question	Could I use your phone?
Would	Formal/polite – question or statement	Would you like a drink? I would like a glass of water.

Ability

Can/cannot	Present ability	He can ski. He cannot surf.
Could/could not	Past ability Option – polite or ability	He could ski when he was young. We could ski, or we could snowboard.

Possibility

May/may not	Moderate future possibility	The bus may be here in five minutes.
Might/might not	Moderate present possibility Moderate future possibility	The bus might be here soon. The bus might be here in five minutes.
Should/should not	Stronger possibility	The bus should be here soon.
Must/must not	Certainty	The bus must be here by now.
Will/will not	Future certainty	The bus will arrive at 9 pm.

Suggestions/Obligation

Should/should not	Recommendation Duty (Can be refused)	You should eat at that new restaurant. I should go to the party, but I am sick.
Ought to / ought not to	Necessity (ethical)	Leaders ought to set a good example.
Must	Necessity (personal feeling)	I must study harder if I want to pass.
Must not	Negative law	Passengers must not bring guns on planes.
Have to *** (Need to)	Necessity (from an outside source - parents, teachers, boss, law, reason)	My teacher said I have to study harder. I have to write a quiz today. Korean drivers have to wear seatbelts.
Do not have to ***	Not necessary	Cyclists do not have to wear a helmet.
(Had) better (not) ***	Warning	You better write the quiz, or you will fail. You better not swim in shark infested water.

***These phrases are not modal verbs, but they are often used in a similar way as modal verbs.

Activity 1

Fill in the blanks with the appropriate word(s).

Hyun Gee has a weight problem. He knows that he ____________________ eat fresh fruits and vegetables instead of instant or fatty food, and he ______________ eat healthy food because he lives in the countryside; however, he prefers to eat junk food every day. Because his father died early from a heart attack, he has always known that he _________________ have heart problems in the future. However, yesterday he went to the doctor who told him that he ____________ start eating better because his health is in serious trouble. In fact, the doctor said that he __________________ lose weight immediately, and he _________________ eat any more fast food, or he _________________ have a heart attack within the next few months. Needless to say, now Hyun Gee knows how serious the situation is, and he also feels that he ________________ lose weight.

When Ga Eun started her job, she was told that she ________________ work overtime unless she wanted to do extra work. She was also told that she ____________________ be able to get a promotion within six months like more than two thirds of her other coworkers. However, she now realizes that if her boss asks her if she _______________________ work overtime, it really means that she ____________________ work late regardless of whether or not she has other plans. She now also knows that she ______________________ never complain about her work hours because then she most certainly _____________________ get a promotion.

Waiter: "Good evening, Sir. ___________________ I take your order?"

Customer: "Yes, I ____________________ like to order red wine and steak with a side order of salad."

W: "I'm sorry, Sir, but tonight we ___________________ serve that dish because we are out of steak. You ____________________ order grilled chicken, or you ___________________ have oysters instead."

C: "Unfortunately, I _____________________ eat oysters because I'm allergic to them, so I guess I _______________________________ order the grilled chicken."

W: "___________________ you like to order dessert now?"

C: "I ___________________ have dessert later, but I'm not sure yet."

W: "Very well, Sir. I ___________________ be back in a moment with your wine."

Activity 2

Using the modal verb and conditional lessons, answer the questions in full conditional sentences.

Example: Hyun Young got lost driving to the beach. What could she have done to have avoided getting lost?

Possible Answer: If I had been Hyun Young, I would have used my GPS.

1. Hyun Seok lost a million won gambling at the casino. What could he have done with that money?

____

2. A business owner needs to cut costs. What usually happens in this situation?

____

3. Elizabeth did not like her new boss, so she quit her job immediately. Are there any other ways she might have solved her problem?

____

4. Moon Soon just found a diamond ring on the street. If you were her, what would you do?

____

5. A student went out drinking the night before his exam. What usually happens in this situation?

____

6. Seung Ho is watching two teenagers beat up a homeless man. If you were him, what would you do?

____

7. Min Kyoung has a blind date tomorrow. What do you think might happen?

____

8. A twelve-year-old boy runs away from home. What might happen to him?

____

9. Young Jun forgot to lock the door when he left home. What could happen to his house?

____

6 Adjectives

Adjectives are descriptive words which modify or give more details about nouns.

Example: I have a car.
Example: I have a shiny new black car.

In the above example, the adjectives are in front of the noun; however, adjectives can follow nouns if you use sense verbs (smell, taste, look, etc.) or verbs of being (be, seem).

Example: The car looked shiny and new.

Grammar Tip

As in most English grammar rules, there are some exceptions to adjective order, most notably, words, titles, or phrases which have been influenced by French.

Example: Boutros Boutros Ghali is the former Secretary General of the United Nations.

Adjective order

When using more than one adjective, it is important to know the order in which they should be placed.

Determiner	Characteristic	Physical Description				Origin	Material	Qualifier
		Size	Shape	Age	Color			
three	funny	big	flat	old	red	Kenyan	wood	baseball
a	shiny	small	square	new	blue	Western	gold	computer
some	sweet	tiny	round	one year old	pink	British	glass	sports
many	terrifying	huge	spherical	vintage	white	Cartier	leather	homemade

Grammar Tip

In general, writers should not use more than three adjectives (not including the determiner) in a row to describe a noun.

Examples: Three funny old baseball players were teaching children how to play the game.
A shiny new gold watch was lying on the ground.
Some sweet British grandmothers raised money to help homeless dogs.
Many terrifying huge white dogs attacked me.

Grammar Tip

If there are two adjectives of the same type, the order does not matter, but they should be separated by a comma.

Example: The crunchy, sweet cookies were homemade.
Example: The sweet, crunchy cookies were homemade.

Activity 1

Identify the adjectives in the sentence and their type. Then correct the sentence if it is in the wrong order.

1. The actress famous lived in a brick modest simple home.

____

2. Yoon Jin's loud annoying parrot lives in a black metal enormous cage.

____

3. Paul told his friends about the ferocious puppy Dalmatian.

____

4. The ancient German castle sat empty in the open field.

____

5. Donna brought back silk from India flowing soft.

____

6. A black ugly old cat scared me when it jumped from the window to the ground.

____

7. I could not study because there were noisy four women laughing loudly.

____

8. Ainsley's fiancé gave her a ring diamond expensive Tiffany.

____

9. These kiwis green New Zealand are both tangy and sweet.

____

10. The students journalism decided to start new campus a newspaper.

____

Adjective Clauses

Adjective clauses are dependent clauses which modify nouns to give more information or to clarify a noun.

Example: Blizzards are dangerous storms which include high winds and heavy snowfall.

Relative Pronouns

Adjective clauses always require relative pronouns. The following chart organizes the type of relative pronoun, and its place or function in a sentence.

Function	People	Things	Place	Time	Explanation
Subject	Who, that	Which, that			
Object	That, whom	Which, that	Where, which	when	What, why
Possessive	Whose	Whose, of which			

Example:
Is that the person who stole your wallet? (subject)
Is that the person whom you mugged? (object)
Is that the person whose wallet was stolen? (possessive)

Grammar Tip

When talking about a place, "which" is more formal than "where," and "whom" is generally more formal than "that" in English sentences.

Example: "There is the place where she met her husband." (informal)
Example: "There is the place at which she met her husband" (formal)

Similarly, "that" is more often used in informal English than "who" (for people) or "which" (for things). However, "that" is the preferred relative pronoun in two cases.

1. Indefinite pronouns
Example: I told him to pack **everything** that fits in the suitcases.

2. Nouns modified by superlatives
Example: He is **the fastest** runner that the world has ever seen.

Types of Adjective Clauses

There are two types of adjective clauses, the restrictive relative clause and the non-restrictive relative clause.

Restrictive Relative Clause

Example: A farmer is a person who grows crops and raises livestock.

Non-Restrictive Relative Clause

Example: Julie's farm, which had been owned by her family for a century, was sold last week.

Grammar Tip

Commas are not usually used after the relative pronoun in the restrictive relative clause. However, if additional information is given in the non-restrictive relative clause that is not necessary to understand the meaning of the subject of the sentence, then commas are necessary.

My sister, who lives in Ireland, is studying medicine. (one sister)
My sister who lives in Ireland is a student. My sister who lives in Hong Kong is a business person.

Activity 1

Choose the correct relative pronoun for formal writing.

1. Is Lisa the girl __________ dress was ruined?
2. Do you know the actor __________ is the villain in this movie?
3. Eun Joo, ______________ was falsely accused of murder, spent ten years in the jail ______ __________ is located just outside of the city.
4. Is she the one __________ you are going to invite to the party?
5. He is the youngest chef __________ has ever graduated from this cooking academy.
6. Do you know the reason __________ so few people came to this event?
7. George has a car ___________ is always breaking down, but he can take it to his uncle's repair shop ______ is cheaper than other places.

Activity 2

Add commas to the following sentences where appropriate.

1. Glenn is a boy who loves horses.
2. They hired the quiet woman whom the boss interviewed last week.
3. The company which is located on the other side of the street has 532 employees.
4. Gregor's Hamburgers which is the largest restaurant chain in the city was established in 1962.
5. The man whose leg was hurt in a car accident was taken to the hospital by ambulance.
6. Where is the good looking guy whom you want to invite to the party?
7. Robson Motors which is the top ranking car company in the country had to recall thousands of cars last week because of engine problems.
8. The textbook which is on top of Yong Hee's desk is the textbook for this class.
9. *Gray's Anatomy* which has been an extremely important medical textbook for the past 150 years was written by Henry Gray.
10. The house which is located at the end of the street is mine.

Activity 3

Write your own definitions for the following nouns using adjective clauses.

1. Bees

____

2. Mothers

____

3. Passports

____

4. Love

____

5. Education

____

7 Active vs. Passive Voice

One of the first lessons students learn when they begin to study English sentence structure is English sentences are usually ordered this way: subject + verb + object. The subject performs the action, the verb is the action, and the object is the recipient of the action.

Example: The **cat** (subject) **ate** (verb) the **mouse** (object).

This sentence structure is called "active voice," and it is the preferred order for many kinds of writing, especially in the humanities. Nevertheless, a different kind of sentence structure called "passive voice" is also necessary in certain instances.

Example: The mouse was eaten by the cat.
auxiliary verb (form of "to be") + main verb (past participle) + (by) = passive voice

The above example, the object and subject switch places without changing the underlying meaning of the sentence.

Passive use is the preferable form of sentence structure in the following instances:

Situation	Explanation	Example
Scientific reports and papers	Passive voice is considered more objective in science.	Cancerous cells were found in the samples.
Emphasizing an object	Sometimes emphasizing the object is more dramatic, or authors want to emphasize the effect instead of the cause.	Millions of people were killed by the government during the bloody conflict.
Uncertain, unclear, or unknown subject	In some cases, the subject is either unknown or unimportant in the sentence.	The windows were broken around midnight.

Grammar Tip

The auxiliary verb (to be) changes depending on the time period and amount.

The prisoner **was brought** yesterday.
The prisoners **are being brought** in at this moment.
The prisoner **will be brought** in tomorrow.

Activity 1

Change the following active sentences into passive sentences.

1. Most Koreans eat *kimchi*.

____

2. Heavy rain caused a landslide.

____

3. A massive earthquake and tsunami damaged the Fukushima Daiichi nuclear plant in 2011.

____

4. Sir Edmund Hillary and Tenzing Norgay were the first people to successfully reach the summit of Mt. Everest in 1953.

____

5. Kim Yu Na won the gold medal in women's figure skating at the 2010 Winter Olympic Games.

____

Activity 2

Change the following passive sentences into active sentences. If there is no clear actor in the original sentence, use common sense to determine the subject in the active sentence.

1. He was hired for the new position.

____

2. The bathrooms are cleaned at around 1 pm.

____

3. The student was failed for plagiarizing her essay.

____

4. Hangul was developed in the 15th century.

____

5. English is taught in this class.

____

6. Lee Myung Bak was elected as the President of the Republic of Korea in 2008.

____

8 Comparatives and Superlatives

Writers often use adjectives or descriptive words to describe the nouns they are using. Sometimes when there is more than one noun, writers want to talk about differences between the nouns by using comparatives and superlatives.

Comparatives compare two adjectives describing nouns while superlatives show the greatest degree of a characteristic.

Examples:
This dress is more expensive than that dress. (comparative)
This dress is the most expensive in the store. (superlative)

Adjective Modification

Adjectives are modified as comparatives and superlatives based on the amount of syllables or beats in the word.

Examples:
Beautiful - Beau/ti/ful (3 syllables)
More / less beautiful (comparative)
Most / least beautiful (superlative)

Sweet (1 syllable)
Sweeter (comparative)
Sweetest (superlative)

However, students should be careful because English words are often incorporated into Korean or pronounced by Koreans with a different amount of syllables.

Example:
Cute: Cute (English - 1 syllable) verses Cue/tuh (Korean - 2 syllable)

Therefore, students need to make sure they are sounding out syllables with English pronunciation before they modify adjectives.

Constructing Comparatives and Superlatives

Rule	Comparative Form	Superlative Form
1 syllable ending in "e" fine, wide	Passive voice is considered more objective in science.	Add "st" finest, widest
1 syllable ending in 1 vowel and 1 consonant hot, sad	Double the consonant + "er" hotter, sadder	Double the consonant +est hottest, saddest
1 syllable ending in more than 1 consonant or vowel strange, cool	Add + "er" stranger, cooler	Add "est" strangest, coolest
2 syllables ending in "y" silly, funny	"y" ⇨ "i" + "er" sillier, funnier	"y" ⇨ "i" + "est" silliest, funniest
2 syllables or more (not ending in "y") beautiful, expensive	Add "more" more beautiful, more expensive	Add "most" most beautiful, most expensive

Word	Comparative Form	Superlative form
clever	cleverer/more clever	cleverest/most clever
gentle	gentler/more gentle	gentlest/most gentle
friendly	friendlier/more friendly	friendliest/most friendly
quiet	quieter/ more quiet	quietest/most quiet
simple	simpler/more simple	simplest/most simple

The following adjectives are irregular and do not follow the previously given rules.

Word	Comparative Form	Superlative Form
good	better	best
bad	worse	worst
far	farther	farthest
little	less	least
many	more	most

Signpost See page 130 for information about the definite article and superlatives.

Activity 1

Read the following passages and modify the following words as appropriate.

At first glance, it does not seem that Hyea Su is a unique student. She is not beautiful, cute, or tall student in the class. She is smart, but there are other students who are smart than her. Similarly, when playing sports, she is not the fast or the slow student, and half of the class can run far than her in little time than she can run. However, Hyea Su is a very funny girl, and she tells the good jokes and stories her friends have ever heard. Her classmates think that one day she may become famous comedian in Korea because of her great sense of humor.

Andy wanted to buy a new car. He was not looking for the cheap car or the expensive car but for a mid-priced vehicle. Initially, the car salesperson showed him a red car and a black car. The red car accelerated fast and had good features than the black car, but the black car was many fuel efficient and had a sleek design than the other car. Andy could not decide which car was good. Finally, the salesperson showed him a white car. It was a bit expensive than the other two, but in every other way, it was the good of the three cars. In the end, Andy drove home happy in his brand new white car.

9 Using Non-English Words in English

What is the difference between a sundae and *sundae*?

Using italics helps the reader to understand the difference between an English term and a word from another language. Using Korean, Chinese, or words from any other language is perfectly acceptable in English assignments as long as the word is written and explained properly.

Step 1: Romanize the word

Words written in other scripts need to be written in Roman characters.

비빔밥 → bibimbap
月饼 → yue bing

Step 2: Italics and capitalization

Non-English general nouns need to be italicized and left in lower case letters if they have not been accepted into the English language.

bibimbap → *bibimbap*
yue bing → *yue bing*

Signpost See page 133 for more information on proper and general nouns.

If these words are written by hand, they should be underlined.
bibimbap → <u>bibimbap</u>

Proper nouns should not be italicized, and the first letter of each word should be capitalized.
Seoul → Seoul
kim eun jee → Kim, Eun Jee

Step 3: Define and incorporate into a sentence

Writers should never assume their readers know non-English words; therefore, general nouns need to be explained or defined the first time they are used. Non English words should also conform to English grammar rules.

Bibimbap is a Korean dish that consists of mixed rice, vegetables, egg, and red pepper paste.
Yue bing is a traditional Chinese dessert that is eaten during the Mid-Autumn Festival.

Grammar Tip

If a non-English word has an easy translation, use the appropriate English word.

She wore a beautiful *jinju* necklace. → She wore a beautiful pearl necklace.

Activity 1

Change the following words into Roman script and decide if these words should be italicized (underline) or capitalized.

막걸리	고추장	고시원	김치찌개
삼겹살	설날	호떡	대구시
대구	성균관대학교	上海	餃子

Activity 2

Now use simple adjective clauses to define these words in a sentence.

막걸리 ______________________________

고추장 ______________________________

삼겹살 ______________________________

김치찌개 ______________________________

호떡 ______________________________

설날 ______________________________

餃子 ______________________________

Signpost See page 148 for more information on simple adjective clauses.

Activity 3

Using the space provided, rewrite one of the following paragraphs using the steps previously covered.

추석 is a wonderful way to experience unique aspects of Korean culture. For instance, food is a very important part of the holiday. For dinner, Koreans usually eat 불고기 and 잡채. They also eat 송편 or drink 식혜 after the main meal. Many families also engage in tradition when they perform 차례 by a special table set with offerings of food such as 밥, 과일, and 생선. Sometimes families will even dress in 한복 for this activity. Finally, some Koreans still enjoy watching 씨름 matches during the vacation period. Thus, 추석 is a great way to understand traditional Korean culture.

北京 is a great place to travel on vacation. First, 毛澤東's tomb is an important place to visit to understand the history of China, and 万里长城 is located close to the city, allowing visitors to visit it easily. In addition, many kinds of food are found throughout the city. 北京烤鸭 is the most famous. However, 烙饼 is also a quick snack tourists can enjoy. Finally, no trip is complete without a trip to the 京剧. Therefore, if tourists want a fun-filled destination where they can eat local delicacies, they should visit 北京.

10 Academic Writing Techniques

Although English grammar is more or less standardized, there are many different types and styles of writing which use, allow, or prohibit particular techniques. In university, the two most common forms of writing are personal reflection and academic writing. Personal reflection writing might be used to analyze student teaching experiences in education classes, reflect on field trips, or respond to movies watched in class. It tends to give subjective, personal, and direct opinions and thoughts. On the other hand, academic writing is more objective, structured, and formal. Students discussing policies, reporting on experiments they have conducted, or analyzing laws should use academic English writing techniques. Here are examples of the two types of writing.

Personal Reflection Example:

During practice teaching on Wednesday, one of my students was talking very loudly to his friend, so I asked him to be quiet. However, he swore at me and told me that my lesson was too boring. When I was younger, teachers would have dealt with that behavior with corporal punishment; however, these days teachers in Seoul are not allowed to use these kinds of punishment. I did not know how to act without corporal punishment, but I told him that he had to stay after class and talk to me. I was a little bit afraid, but I talked to the student individually and asked him why he had acted that way. Away from his friends, he seemed more ashamed and told me about some problems in his life. Hitting the student would have been a faster way to discipline him, but I think we developed a better relationship by talking about the problem.

Academic Writing Example:

In November 2010, Kwak, No Hyun, the head of the Seoul Metropolitan Office of Education (SMOE), implemented new regulations banning corporal punishment in the city's schools. Previous to the ban, many Korean teachers had used varying forms of physical punishment such as push–ups or hitting in order to discipline students. Many teachers are worried about the effectiveness of non-physical punishment while others have little experience using alternative forms of discipline. However, there are other types of punishment which work just as well or better than corporal punishment, and this paper will examine the benefits of these alternatives.

The first type of writing is perfectly acceptable in certain situations, but sometimes a more formal academic style is necessary to examine a topic more objectively. The following section will help you to understand the writing techniques which are not acceptable in academic writing, and it will also show you simple ways of changing personal writing into more objective language.

Activity 1

What are some differences in the above examples' styles and the words used?

Academic Writing

Do not use the following writing techniques when writing academic or formal assignments.

Problem	Correction
Coordinating Conjunctions • Replace with transitions at the beginning of a sentence	~~So this method is effective~~. Thus, this method is effective.
Abbreviations	~~Tv~~ – Television
Acronyms • Do not use an acronym unless you first write out the full term and put the acronym in brackets	Post – Traumatic Stress Disorder (PTSD)
Truncations	~~Sat.~~ – Saturday
Contractions	~~Won't~~ – Will not ~~They're~~ – They are
Slang/Informal Language Texting ***Emoticons should never be used***	~~Wanna~~ – Want to ~~C u soon~~ – See you soon ~~*^^*~~
Singular Nouns • Replace with plural nouns when talking about things in general	~~An apple is crunchier than an orange.~~ Apples are crunchier than oranges.
Gender Exclusive Language • Do not use pronouns, terms, or expressions which exclude a gender	~~Mankind~~ – Humankind ~~Fireman~~ - Firefighter ~~If a child misbehaves, he should be punished.~~ If children misbehave, they should be punished.
Etc./and so on/…	~~Carrots, cucumbers, etc. have many vitamins.~~ Vegetables such as carrots or cucumbers have many vitamins.
Konglish/Sinicized English	~~I have a promise tonight.~~ I have plans/an appointment tonight.
Digits • Do not use digits for numbers nine and under, rounded numbers, or numbers at the beginning of sentences (with the exception of dates)	~~There were 8 students in class.~~ There were eight students in class.

Tip You should use digits if you are using unrounded numbers above 10, percentages, dates, eras, fractions, money, decimals, surveys, scores, or other types of specific numbers.

Activity 2

Rewrite the following sentences to correct the inappropriate academic language.

1. SKKU was the first uni in Korea when it opened in thirteen ninety eight. At first, SKKU focused on teaching material related only to Confucianism, but now students can study film, Russian, engineering, etc.

____

____

____

2. Seon Ah's doggie died in Feb. after being pretty sick for a looooong time. ㅜㅜ

____

____

____

3. On Thurs. a policeman is needed to man the gate at the festival because there's gonna be people who think it's okay to bring alcohol into a children's event.

____

____

____

4. Dae Hui's aircon had been broken for 5 days in 38 degree weather. But he couldn't call a repair guy to fix it because his handphone was also broken.

____

____

5. If a student is late for the quiz, test, exam, and so on, he will not be allowed extra time to complete it. And he will also lose participation marks cause he was not in class for the full time.

____

____

Using Certain Pronouns

When writing high level academic papers, it is sometimes appropriate for advanced students to use personal pronouns; however, when learning how to write, students should try to avoid:

I/Me/My/Mine	Direct personal opinion should be replaced with research or logical arguments.	~~I think this cancer drug is effective.~~ Research shows this cancer drug is effective.
You/Your/Yours	In some cases, using 'you' may be inappropriate or offensive to the audience.	~~You should not get divorced~~. People should not get divorced.
We/Our/Ours	Academic writing should be used to communicate to a wide audience not just to your particular group.	~~In our culture, we eat *kimchi*.~~ In Korea, Koreans eat *kimchi*.
I/We vs. You Us vs. Them	Try to avoid language which unnecessarily polarizes groups.	~~We have different views than those people.~~ Students have different views than teachers.

Writers should also avoid asking simple questions or posing questions directly to their readers.

Asking the reader a direct question. • The reader cannot respond to your question while reading. In addition, it is the responsibility of the writer to give information to the reader.	Why do you think junk food is harmful?
Answering a simple question immediately. • Concise writing is better in short assignments. Additionally, it is better to prove your argument with evidence	Is junk food unhealthy? Yes, junk food is unhealthy.
Giving an answer as an incomplete sentence. • Sentence fragments should not occur in academic writing	Is junk food unhealthy? Yes.

The questions given above could be rephrased as the following statements:

Give your reader answers instead of posing new questions.	~~Why do you think junk food is harmful~~? Junk food is harmful because it contains an excess of calories and fat.
State your position clearly in one sentence where possible.	~~Is junk food unhealthy? Yes, junk food is unhealthy.~~ ~~Is junk food unhealthy? Yes.~~ Junk food is unhealthy for a number of reasons. Junk food is unhealthy because it contributes to heart disease and diabetes.

Activity 3

Make corrections to the following sentences. For instance, change the pronouns into nouns that are clearer and more objective in academic writing, or make the questions into statements.

1. Should you send your child to an English kindergarten?

____

____

2. We have been told we should not smoke, but do you know the reasons why we should not smoke?

____

____

3. Do you think multiculturalism is good for our society?

____

____

4. I think Korea is a safe country because I feel safe walking around late at night.

____

____

5. Are there any benefits to living on a farm? Yes.

____

____

6. Why do you think there is global warming?

____

____

11 Logical Fallacies

When presenting an argument, it is vital to be logical and this requires an understanding of common logical mistakes. The following are logical fallacies that can often be found in articles, essays and arguments. Familiarity with them will help you to avoid them in your own work and identify them in information presented to you. Match the definitions with the names in the box.

1.____________________________: **The writer relies on the status of someone who agrees with their opinion as evidence that they are right.** Using the name of a well-respected or successful person to support your argument is only appropriate if they are qualified to speak with authority on the topic. Remember that sometimes authorities are wrong so using a respected name does not prove that you are right.

2.____________________________: **The writer criticizes the person who has the opposite opinion instead of the reasons for their opinion.** Remember that even bad people can be right, and not liking someone is not a reason to think they are wrong.

3.____________________________: **The writer compares the main idea to something else, but the comparison is weak or inappropriate.** Analogies are very useful to help make a point clear, but they must match the relevant details of the topic.

4.____________________________: **The writer assumes that only two opinions are possible, usually a good one and a bad one.** They do not consider ideas in the middle of the two extremes or any other possible opinions.

5.____________________________: **The writer uses their conclusion or opinion to support the premise.** In other words, the premise is the same as the conclusion.

6.____________________________: **The writer confuses correlation for cause and effect.** They connect two events by saying that the second must have been caused by the first. Of course, while outcomes are caused by preceding events, the time sequence doesn't prove causation.

7.____________________________: **The writer assumes that one event or action will lead to far more serious events.** The aim is usually to scare the reader. Remember that the more serious actions on the slope are things that most people can still choose to avoid and are not really inevitable outcomes of choosing the milder action.

8.____________________________: **The writer explains the opposite viewpoint but adds or removes details to make it seem weaker or ridiculous.** The aim is to pretend to have considered the other side, but really to have misrepresented it. Remember to research opposing opinions by reading what the opponents really say, and when you use a counterargument in your writing, give appropriate context so you present the ideas accurately.

9.____________________________: **The writer says that if you can't disprove something then it must be true.** This might be that the writer has not seen evidence against their own position, or it could be that their opponents have not definitively shown that the idea is true or false. This is a form of shifting the burden of proof, or saying that the writer's opinion is right and the evidence is the lack of evidence against it.

10.____________________________: **The writer says that an idea is right because it is popular.** Of course, lots of popular ideas are wrong and it can be hard to gauge popularity. A hundred people might seem to make an idea popular, but not if there are a million who oppose them.

Argument from authority	Faulty analogy
Argument from ignorance	Bandwagon
False dichotomy	Begging the question
Ad hominem	Slippery slope
Post hoc ergo propter hoc	Straw man

Activity 1

Read the following paragraph and identify the logical fallacies.

Games of Death

Violent video games should be banned because they cause people to be violent. Society has become so obsessed with video games that people are either obsessive gamers or they want video games to be banned. Gamers say that video games do not cause violence, which means they think that games are good for people and everyone should play video games. Psychologist Christine Ferguson says that her research shows no clear link between video games and violence, although she cannot know about violence because she has a good job and lives in a safe neighborhood. Furthermore, her research did not include all violent games, and she did not study the effects on all children, so it does not prove that violent games never make anyone violent. She says that her children are allowed to play violent games, but would she let her children play with real guns or take drugs? If people let their children play violent video games, then they will let them play with real guns, and eventually children will be allowed to kill people in real life. John Ryan, a retired police officer, saw lots of violence in his career, so his opinion is stronger than that of a psychologist. Ryan is convinced that video games cause violence, and he says, "My three grandsons play shooting games, and they fight with each other all the time, so the connection is clear." He goes on to say, "If they play video games at night, they will probably fight with each other the next day." An online poll of concerned parents recently showed that 60% of people agree that violence is linked to video games, and this strongly supports my call for violent games to be banned. In conclusion, since people like me think that violent games should be banned, violent games must be dangerous to society; therefore such video games should be banned.

1) Underline the logical fallacies in the paragraph and identify each one with the appropriate number from the list on page 164.

____

____

2) What other logical fallacies do you know? Discuss them with your partner and give some examples.

____

____

Activity 2

In your notebook, write a paragraph of your own including some logical fallacies. Exchange your writing with your partner and try to identify the logical fallacies they have used.

12 Paraphrasing and Summarizing

In academic writing, writers often integrate information from other sources in order to support their own ideas and opinions. Paraphrasing and summarizing are ways of incorporating ideas from other sources without using the exact words.

What is paraphrasing?

Paraphrasing is rewording and rearranging the content of text without changing the meaning or dramatically alerting the length. It is useful alternative to a direct quotation when using information from another source, and it is a valuable skill that is used in the writing process.

Example:
Original text (21 words)

Soccer star Wayne Rooney is a machine designed for sport. His stocky, powerful physique makes him more powerful than his opponents.

Paraphrase version (23 words)

Wayne Rooney, a famous soccer player, has a powerful body which makes him a stronger soccer player than the players he competes against.

Summary version (10 words)
Wayne Rooney's powerful body has made him a soccer legend.

How to paraphrase

There are three main steps in the processes of paraphrasing:

Step 1: Identify key information.

Step 2: Find synonyms.

Step 3: Change the sentence structure or word order.

Example 2:
Original text

An article in *GQ* magazine reports that actor David DeMotto is considering retirement from the movie business due to an undisclosed medical condition.

Step 1: Identify key information

Read the text carefully and highlight or underline the important words to change.

An article in *GQ* magazine **reports** that **actor** David DeMotto is **considering** retirement from the **movie business** due to an **undisclosed medical condition**.

Step 2: Find synonyms

Report	rumour, state, disclose, reveal
Actor	film star, thespian, performer, player
Considering	thinking about, contemplating, planning on
Movie business	film industry, acting
Undisclosed	unnamed, unidentified, secret
Medical condition	health problem, personal reason

New sentence:
An article in *GQ* magazine reveals that film star David DeMotto is thinking about retirement from the film industry due to health problems.

Step 3: Change the sentence structure or word order

Paraphrase 1:
Film star David DeMotto is thinking about retirement from the film industry due to health problems, according to an article in *GQ* magazine.

Paraphrase 2:
Due to health problems, film star David DeMotto is thinking about retirement from the film industry, according to an article in *GQ* magazine.

Signpost See page 16-22 for more information on sentence types.

Activity 1

Rewrite the following sentences by following steps 1–3.

1. The little boy named Sam was very nervous about his test; as a result, he vomited.

2. The rural school could not afford to buy new computers, for they were not cheap.

3. Although Nak Kyun stayed up all night writing his essay, he had too many grammar mistakes to get a good mark.

4. Children between the ages of 9 and 12 study for an average of five hours every week outside of normal school hours.

5. It is against the law for teachers to use corporal punishment in schools in New Zealand.

6. Learning English is very important for entrance into good schools and more opportunities in the workplace.

7. *FourFourTwo* magazine has described Park, Ji Sung as one of the most important players in the English Premier League.

8. South Korean boy band 2PM has signed a new contract with JYP Entertainment.

What is summarizing?

Like paraphrasing, summarizing involves rewording and rearranging the content of a text without changing the meaning, but the writer dramatically reduces the length to provide an overview of the original text. This is particularly useful when a writer wishes to focus on the main idea without including examples, statistics, and details.

How to summarize

There are three main steps in the processes of summarizing:

Step 1: Highlight main points.

Step 2: Remove extra details.

Step 3: Use main points to create an overview.

Example:
Original text (113 words)

Soccer star Wayne Rooney is a machine designed for sports. His stocky, powerful physique makes him more powerful than his opponents. At a height of 176 centimetres, Rooney has a low centre of gravity which enables him to a change direction quickly at pace and outmanoeuvre bigger defenders. His upper body strength is a considerable asset and allows him to hold-off other players while controlling the ball. Although not gifted with electric pace, Rooney's leg strength allows him to kick the ball with significant force which is a great asset as a striker. As a result of these physical attributes and never-say-die attitude, Rooney is considered one of the best players in the game.

Step 1: Highlight the main points

Soccer star **Wayne Rooney** is a machine designed for sports. His stocky, powerful physique makes him **more powerful than his opponents**. At a height of 176 centimetres, Rooney has a **low centre of gravity** which enables him to a change direction quickly at pace and outmanoeuvre bigger defenders. His **upper body strength** is a considerable asset and allows him to hold-off other players while controlling the ball. Although not gifted with electric pace, Rooney's **leg strength** allows him to kick the ball with significant force which is a great asset as a striker. As a result of these physical attributes and never-say-die attitude, Rooney is considered **one of the best players** in the game.

Step 2: Remove extra details

Wayne Rooney
more powerful than his opponents
low centre of gravity
upper body strength
leg strength
one of the best players

Step 3: Use the main points to write an overview
Summary version (10 words)

Wayne Rooney's powerful body has made him a soccer legend.

Activity 2

Now try to summarize the following information into one sentence using steps 1-3.

The rate of birth in South Korea fell to the second lowest in the world. Only Hong Kong has a lower birthrate. There are many reasons why so many couples hesitate to have children. One problem is that there are not enough childcare facilities in Korea. The other issue is that education costs for children are on the rise.

____

____

____

Although Korean adults have one of the lowest levels of obesity in the world, Korean children are getting heavier. A recent study from the Institute for Childhood Nutrition shows 1 in 10 children are obese, and a larger number are overweight. Because of the university entrance exam, even young students spend an increasing amount of time sitting in their chairs studying at home, at afterschool programs, and at their regular public schools. In addition, instead of a diet full of fresh vegetables and fruit, children today eat more junk or instant food than ever before. *Ramyeon*, chips, frozen pre-prepared meals, and hamburgers or French fries have now replaced well balanced, homemade meals for children.

____

____

____

Activity 3

Use the four summarizing steps to make each paragraph into one sentence.

Homeschooling

There are several different reasons why students are homeschooled. Some religious families feel that their children need an education that is more focused on their beliefs. Other parents are worried about negative influences in public schools such as smoking, drugs, bullying, or other forms of violence. There are also children who do not fit in with the regular school system because they are either gifted children who learn faster than regular students or because they have learning disabilities or learn slower than other students. Thus, there is no one reason why parents decide to homeschooled their children.

____

____

Because homeschooling is so different from public schools, some people have concerns about children learning at home. Unlike mainstream schools where children are exposed to a diversity of people and opinions from different teachers and interacting with other students, homeschooled children have only their parents' perspectives or the curriculum's perspective, which was probably chosen by the parents. In addition, children might not be well socialized with mainstream society. As a result, homeschooled children might not be able to fit well into the rest of the community later in life.

____

____

Despite these problems, there are also benefits to homeschooling. First, children who are very talented or are experiencing learning disabilities can learn at their own pace at home. Children who excel at languages, science, or other subjects can devote more time to their area or areas of interest, and those students may one day be great linguists or scientists because of their extra studies; on the other hand, students who are struggling in one area can devote more time to reading skills, mathematics, or whatever subject they need to improve. The second advantage is that children can have a closer relationship with their parents because they spend much more time with their parents than in the traditional education system. Likewise, parents who teach their children are much more involved in their education, and they can help guide their children in life and education.

____

____

Tip

If paraphrasing or summarizing from another source, you must include an in-text citation in order to indicate clearly where you found the original information. See page 175-176 for more information on in-text citations.

Research Skills

Students often hear that they should not plagiarize or copy someone else's work, but they do not always have the skills to avoid replicating previously published work. This section gives students practical skills to both avoid plagiarism and make their writing assignments stronger by incorporating outside evidence into their work. Students will first learn what plagiarim is and how they can correctly incorporate in-text citations and quotations. Finally, they will learn how to cite sources used in their writing.

This section covers:

- Research and Writing
- In-Text Citations
- Quotations
- Works Cited

1 Research and Writing

In academic writing, it is not enough just to provide your own ideas and opinions. Good academic writing involves the development of the writer's ideas with support from other credible authors and sources.

When writers provide information from other sources, they must provide the reader with proper documentation of all the information used. If writers take information without acknowledging it, they are guilty of plagiarism.

What is plagiarism?

Plagiarism is taking information and ideas from other sources and claiming them to be yours. By not acknowledging the source(s), the writer is committing literary theft.

In example 1, Student A has taken information from the author H.J. Chang but has not acknowledged it. The writer is claiming that the idea is his/her own. This is plagiarism.

Example 1: Culture influences a country's economic performance. A particular culture may produce people with certain behavioral traits.

In example 2, the student has correctly acknowledged the original author and avoided plagiarism.

Example 2: According to H.J. Chang, Professor of Economics at Cambridge University, "Culture influences a country's economic performance. At a given point in time, a particular culture may produce people with particular behavioral traits that are more conducive to achieving certain goals, including economic development, than other countries" (200).

Writers are also guilty of plagiarism if they attempt to paraphrase too closely (put into your own words) information from another source. In example 3, while the writer does not use the exact words from the author, the paraphrase is too closely related to the original. Again, the source is not cited.

Example 3: Culture can affect **a country's economic performance**. Over time, **a particular culture may produce people with** certain **behavior traits**.

How can writers avoid plagiarism?

When using information from other sources, the source(s) must always be acknowledged. By providing an accurate and full description of the sources used, the writer can avoid plagiarism. This is done in two ways:

1. By providing a parenthetical citation, called an **in-text citation**, within the text. This is where the author's name and page number is provided in parenthesis at the end of the borrowed information (MLA Style).

> **Example 1**: The Maori language spoken by the indigenous people of New Zealand is closely related to Hawaiian Tahitian (Tane 196).

In this example, the reader can see the information came from page 196 and is written by the author Tane.

2. By providing a **Works Cited** page at the end of the writing that provides the reader a more comprehensive record of the source.

> **Example 2**: Tane, John. *The History of the Maori Language*. Wellington: Whitcombe and Tombs, 2006.

In the Works Cited page, the reader can find out the full name of the author, the title of the source, and the publishing details.

Is there a format or style that I should follow when making in-text citations and a Works Cited page?

Depending on whom you are writing for and the type of writing you are doing, different documentation styles can be used. Below are just a few of the many styles used in writing:

- APA Style (American Psychological Association)
- Chicago Style
- Harvard Style
- MLA Style (Modern Language Association)

This book will follow the MLA Style; however, it is important to check with your professor or department to find out which style they prefer or use.

2 In-Text Citations

How do I create an in-text citation?

In an in text citation, the works of others are acknowledged using a parenthetical citation. This involves placing the name(s) of the author(s), page number(s), or both in parentheses ( ).
An in-text citation gives the reader a trail to follow should they wish to find out more information on the source(s) used in the text.

1. Basic entry: Place the author(s)'s last name(s) and/or page number(s) in parenthesis at the end of the sentence.

Example 1: When developing countries are faced with a payment crisis, "Signing an agreement with the IMF is crucial" (Chang 145).

Example 2: According to Chang, "Signing an agreement with the IMF is crucial," when developing countries are faced with a payment crisis (145).

If the reader wants more information on the source he or she can go to the works cited page and find the full reference:

Chang, Ha Joon. *Bad Samaritans: The Myth of Free Trade and the Secret History of Capitalism*. New York: Bloomsbury Press, 2008.

2. A source with multiple authors: If a source has multiple authors, state the names. If the source has three authors or less, list the author's last names as they appear with the page number. With more than three authors, you can either use the first authors name followed by et al., or cite them all.

Example 3: The Arabica coffee bean is commonly used for breakfast blends because of its moderate aroma and body (Kim, Modeno, and Yang 31).

3. Authors with same last names: If the authors have the same last names, use the first initials of both authors.

Example 4: The authors state, "Tougher laws are necessary to battle the growing social problems associated with drugs in South Korea" (J.H. Kim, T.K. Kim 3).

Example 5: S.H. Park argues that tougher drug laws are vital in fighting the battle against crime (17). This view is also supported by Seoul metropolitan police who reported that drug related crimes have increased by 7% from the last year (J.S. Park 27).

4. Internet source: If using an Internet source with an author and page number, follow the standard for basic entry. If the author or page number is absent, include the first item that appears in the Works Cited entry (article name, website name).

Example 6: After the recent data hacking attacks at SK Telecom, many people are nervous about placing personal information online (Kim, "Time to Hit Reset Button").

Do not include the URLs in-text unless it is the only way to signal the entry in the Works Cited. If using the URL, just provide the name of the site like BBC.com or CNN.com

5. No author: If the author is not known, use the title of the work instead of the author.

Example 7: During the 17th century, Seoul began to emerge as an important trade center due to its strategic location ("Seoul History" 4).

Source	Citation
1 author	(Kim 123)
Multiple authors	(Kim and Park 123) (Kim, Lee, and Park 123) (Kim et.al 123)
Authors with the same last name	(J.H. Kim, T.K. Kim 3)
Internet source	If author and page number (Kim 123) No author or page number ("article name")
No author	(Book *title* 123) ("Article title" 123)

3 Quotations

What is a quotation?

A quotation is essentially the acknowledgement of words and ideas from another author or source. They can either be the exact words taken from another person(s) (direct quotation) or the summarization from an author or source (indirect quotation).

When should I use a quotation?

Both direct and indirect quotations can be valuable tool in strengthening your own writing but should never be over used. The aim is to use quotations to expand or support your own ideas and therefore they should NOT form the majority of your writing or overshadow your own idea.

How do I use a quotation?

There are two steps to using a quotation:

1. Provide a context for the quotation. The quotation should follow and support the idea you have made, or precede and set up the idea or point you wish to make.

2. Acknowledge the source and provide a citation. When information has been taken from another source, the source must be acknowledged by including the authors name and pagination (if available). If a writer fails to acknowledge the source(s), he or she is committing plagiarism.

Example 1: Acknowledging the author(s)
The authors state, "Tougher laws are necessary to battle the growing social problems associated with drugs in South Korea" (J.H.Kim, T.K. Kim 3).

Example 2: Not acknowledging the author = plagiarism
Many people argue that tougher drug laws are vital in fighting the battle against crime. This view is also supported by Seoul Metropolitan Police who reported that drug related crimes have increased by 7% from the last year.

Signpost See page 173 for more information on plagiarism.

What is a direct quotation?

A direct quotation is where the writer takes the exact words from an author and places them in quotation marks (" "). If the writer uses a direct quote, the source must be acknowledged by including the name of the author and the page number of the direct quotation (MLA style).

Read the following paragraph and notice how direct quotations are used to support the writers' own ideas.

Activity 1

Underline any phrases or sentences in quotation marks. Fill in the following table with information from the paragraph.

Understanding Shyness

Shyness is a word often used to describe a sense of discomfort and/or inhibition in social situations. Ray Crozier, author of the book *Understanding Shyness*, says that it can refer to "Both transient experiences and to more stable characteristics of individuals" and classifies the elements of shyness into three categories, "cognitive, somatic, and behavioral" (31). People who are shy often have negative thoughts about themselves and fear negative evaluation of others. Psychologist James Buss states that "Shyness and fear are closely related" (154), and shy people will usually avoid situations where there is a risk to the self. In addition, people who feel shy may exhibit a range of physiological reactions such as trembling and shaking, accelerated heart rate, blushing, sweating, and increased urinary urges. When placed in an uncomfortable situation, P.G. Zimbardo, a professor at Monash University in Melbourne claims, "A person is likely to display a number of different behaviors like speaking in a low voice, avoiding eye contact, and exhibiting passivity to reduce the sense of discomfort" (14). While behavioral and somatic symptoms may differ from person to person, there is no doubt that shyness can be socially debilitating; therefore, care and consideration is needed when dealing with individuals who suffer from shyness.

	Quotation 1	Quotation 2	Quotation 3
Name of author			
Page number			

Supporting the Author

It is often a good idea to provide some support or background information on the author you are citing. Is the author or source an expert in this field? Does the author or source have some title or qualification that makes him or her more qualified and therefore more believable?

Remember, quotations can help to strengthen and support your own ideas; therefore, providing sources that are credible will help your cause.

Activity 2

Fill in the following table with information on the author.

	Quotation 1	Quotation 2	Quotation 3
Background information on author			

Reporting Verbs with Direct and Indirect Quotations

In the paragraph on shyness, in addition to using quotation marks, the writer uses a number of verbs to introduce the quotation. These are called reporting verbs:
The following are some common reporting verbs and phrases:

According to Agree Arque Ask Assert	Claim Declare Define Describe Demonstrate	Emphasize Highlight Identify Insist Indicate	Maintain Mention Predict Propose Recommend	Report Say State Suggest

Activity 3

Look back through the paragraph on shyness and highlight any reporting verbs.

Choosing Reporting Verbs

While it may seem that reporting verbs are similar and can be used with any quotation, the verb that is used is dependent on the type of writing that you are doing.

To make a declarative statement	reports, said, states,
To make a statement where some possibility or other opinion exists	claims, maintains, suggests,
To make an assertive statement	argues, asserts, declares, emphasizes, insists

Rules with Direct Quotations

1. Incorporate the quote into your own sentence, and place the period after the in-text citation (name and page number) when it follows a quotation.

Example 1: Leading language experts at Southern University argue, "The most effective way of testing a learner's pronunciation is to observe and record the learner performing in a variety of situations" (Nation 95).

2. Capitalize the first word in the quotation.

Example 2: Lewis claims, "Play is the mode through which children encounter and explore knowledge" (201).

3. With a broken quotation, capitalize the first word in the first quotation marks, but do not capitalize the first word in the second quotation marks.

Example 3: "Memorization has a place in language learning," says Professor Lee, "but students need opportunities to practice and use their skills to develop true competency" (42).

4. If the quotation includes a question mark, place it before the end mark.

Example 4: Kim asked, "Will the fever for education ever subside in Korea?" (94).

5. When omitting a word, phrase, or sentence from a longer passage, use ellipses (three spaced periods) to tell the reader that the quoted material is part of a longer text.

Example 5: 15% of Japanese schoolchildren have shown signs of video-game addiction, **thought by some psychiatrists to be one of the highest rates in the world**, which is similar with that of South Korea (Barron 171).
Example 6: Psychologist Rolf Barron states, "15% of Japanese schoolchildren have shown signs of video-game addiction...which is similar with that of South Korea" (171).

6. Use only one reporting verb with each quotation.

Incorrect Example 7: According to Malcolm St. John, chairman of Toyota Motors, he **said**, "The new lithium polymer battery pack used in the Samsung T20 will allow higher power density than other cars on the market" (7).

Activity 4

Read the following sentences. If there are any errors, highlight the error and correct it.

1. David Digby mentioned "soon we will be able to send a kangaroo to the moon" (29).

2. "People must learn to live within their means," argued Enes Claw, "If they wish to reduce personal debt.

3. Dr. Rusty Pitt raised an interesting question when he stated, "Are we not all to blame for the increase in global warming"? (45).

4. In a symposium on the role of hip hop music in education, LL Cool J asked, "Successful educational programs for young black inner city children cannot be implemented without first understanding the context......... therefore shouldn't we try to understand hip hop culture"?

5. "I can accept failure, everyone fails at something. But I can't accept not trying," said.

6. John Davis, a man, argues, "We must all take a greater interest in global economics."

7. Jisu Kim, my sixteen year old sister, said, "The world is set for another recession."

8. According to J. H. Chang, author of the book *Bad Samaritans*, "Signing an agreement with the IMF is crucial", when developing countries are faced with a payment crisis (145).

9. According to a report in the Korean Ministry of Commerce, Industry, and Energy, "Korea is set for annual economic growth of 3.5% a year for the next five years" (101).

10. According to a report in the Korean Ministry of Foreign Affairs and Trade, "The EU-South Korean FTA is vital for investment and growth (17)."

Activity 5

In your notebook, write a paragraph that develops the topic given below. Use quotations for support. You do not need to use all the quotations provided.

Topic: University and the influence of peers

Topic sentence: The relationship with peers is critical during university life.

Book 1
Author: Dr. James Kim
Title: *Social Development*

Quotation 1: "University is often a time of considerable uncertainty" (37).

Quotation 2: "Peer influence can be both positive and negative" (49).

Quotation 3: "Having healthy relationships with peers allows for a positive adjustment to university life" (141).

Book 2
Author: Simon Kim, David Parker, and Sarah Lee
Title: *University Drinking Habits*

Quotation 4: "Peer influence is commonly cited as a key factor in the development of excessive drinking habits among university students" (17).

Quotation 5: "Peer groups and university clubs provide active opportunities for young people to interact in a variety of different ways" (18).

Quotation 6: "University policy makers have long debated whether the current drinking habits of freshmen students in Korea are a cause for concern" (36).

Quotation 7: "Alcohol can help relax tension between students and create a bonding experience" (39).

What is an indirect quotation?

An indirect direct quotation is where the writer presents the ideas from an author in the writers own words while staying true to the original idea. Because the writer does not use the exact words from the source, quotation marks are not necessary.

As with direct quotations, the author and source must still be acknowledged as while the words may be your own, the idea is not. Indirect quotations also use reporting verbs, however the subordinator that is often added to the reporting verb.

Example 1: Direct quotation
David Johnson, a leading expert in sports nutrition, argues, "A healthy diet is vital for optimum performance in sport" (34).

Example 2: Indirect quotation
David Johnson, a leading expert in sports nutrition, argues that to perform at the highest level in sports, a good nutritious diet is important (34).

How do we create an indirect quotation?

Indirect quotations are created by paraphrasing and summarizing ideas and text from other sources. Paraphrasing is used with shorter pieces of information such as sentences and phrases. In contrast, summarizing is used when we want to create an overview of a longer text or idea. The main idea is given but not the examples or details.

Signpost See page 166-171 for more information on paraphrasing and summarizing.

Activity 6

In your notebook, write a paragraph that develops the topic given below. Change the direct quotations into indirect quotations for support, and use as many as possible in your paragraph.

Topic: Advertising as a Communication Process
Topic sentence: Advertising is a marketing communications tool

Book 1
Author: Frank Jefkins
Title: *Advertising*
Publisher: Prentice Hall
Date: 2000

Quotation 1: "The object of advertising is usually to change or influence attitudes. It aims to persuade people to buy product A instead of product B, or to promote the habit of continuing to buy A" (15).

Quotation 2: "Advertising is a specialized form of communication because in order to satisfy the marketing function it has to do more than inform. It has to persuade people to complete the marketing strategy which is designed to sell at a profit. Advertising has to influence choice and buying decisions" (13).

Book 2
Author: W. Ronald Lane, Thomas Russell
Title: *Advertising: A Framework*
Publisher: Prentice Hall
Date: 2001

Quotation 3: "Advertising is a primary communications tool of our economic system and our culture. In many respects, advertising reflects the society and contemporary mores in which it functions" (8).

Quotation 4: "Without brands, there would be little or no advertising. Brands allow a consumer to buy a product with an assurance of consistency from one purchase to another. Brand identity is vital as companies try to differentiate their products from a growing number of competitors" (10).

4 Works Cited

How do I create a Works Cited page?

The Works Cited page is the last part of your paper and contains a reference of every source used in the paper.

Look at the following example of a Works Cited page.

Works Cited

Chang, Ha Joon. *Bad Samaritans: The Myth of Free Trade and the Secret History of Capitalism.* New York: Bloomsbury Press, 2008. Print.

Davies, John, Cameron Park, Don DeMotto, and Dave Ferreria. *Capitalism in Africa*. Chicago: Atlas House, 2007. Print.

Gilbert, Nellie. "Money and Power." *Time*. 30 May 2011: 67-71. Print.

South Korea. Ministry of Finance and Economy. Dept. of Fiscal Policy. *Balancing the Books in the New Millennium*. Seoul: 2001. Web. 15 January 2012.

Tanner, Jessie. *The History of Capitalism in Asia*. Tokyo: Discover 21, 2006. Print.

---. *Asia's Economic Miracle.* Tokyo: Discover 21, 2009. Print.

Wray, Praise. "Building a Better Economy." *Journal of Economics*, 20 (2011): pp 237-245.Web. 29 September 2011.

Is there a certain format I should follow?

Like the rest of your writing, the Works Cited page follows a format. The format is as follows:

1. The Works Cited page begins on a new page and is numbered, continuing from the last page in the text.
2. There is a centered title which is one inch from the top of the page. The title is separated from the first entry (source) by two lines.
3. Like the rest of the paper, the Works Cited page has margins.
4. The Works Cited page has a hanging indentation. This means that if an entry is more than one line, the subsequent line(s) is/are indented from the left margin.
5. Double space all entries
6. Entries follow alphabetical order.

Arranging entries in the Works Cited page

1. Book by a single author

Author's last name, first name. *Title of the book*. Publication details. Medium of Publication.

Publication details: Include the city of publication, name of publisher, and the year of publication. Medium of publication: All hard-copy print sources are acknowledged with the word "Print" at the end.

Example 1: Chang, Ha Joon. *Bad Samaritans*: *The Myth of Free Trade and the Secret History of Capitalism*. New York: Bloomsbury Press, 2008. Print.

2. Two or more books by the same author

If citing multiple books from the same author, follow the procedure for a single author for the first entry, and then add three hyphens instead of the authors name for the other books. After the hyphens, add a period, title and publication details

Example 2: Chang, Ha Joon. *Bad Samaritans: The Myth of Free Trade and the Secret History of Capitalism*. New York: Bloomsbury Press, 2008. Print.
---. *Capitalism and Communism*. Seoul: ABC Press, 2006. Print.

3. A book with more than one author

Give the authors details following from how they appear on the title page. For the first name, place it in reverse order as per a single entry but for the other authors; put the names in normal order. Do not put them in alphabetical order unless that is how it is on the title page.

Example 3: Bracken, Daniel, Irene Parker, and Diana Tully. *UFO Abductions*. Sydney: Braeburn House, 1996. Print.

4. An article from a reference book

When citing from an encyclopedia or other reference book, give the author (if present), title, and publication details.

Example 4a: "Shanghai." *The Encyclopedia Britannica*. 4th ed. 2003. Print.

If no author is present then give the title of the section in the reference book and place it in quotation marks. Follow with the title of the reference book, edition, and year.

If citing a specific definition from a dictionary, add the abbreviation Def. (definition) and the appropriate number or letter as found in the dictionary.

Example 4b: "Global Warming." Def.5. *The Oxford Dictionary*. 3rd ed. 1995. Print.

5. A book with no author

If a book has no author, give the title and then publishing details.

Example 5: *New American Standard Bible*. Anaheim, California: Foundation Publications, 1995. Print.

6. Government Publications

Government publications may have many different sources and therefore need to be treated carefully. If no author is given, cite the government that issued it first, and then the agency or department that published it. Finally, follow normal publishing details

Example 6: South Korea. Ministry of Commerce, Industry, and Energy. Dept. of Energy. *Energy in the New Millennium*. Seoul: 2011. Print.

7. A book without publication details

When a book does not have publishing details (place, publisher, or date), include as much information as you can and provide abbreviations for missing information.

n.p. No place of publication provided
n.p. No publisher information provided
n.d. No date provided
n.pag. No pagination provided (no page number given.)

Example 7: Bracken, Daniel, Irene Parker, and Diana Tully. *UFO Abductions*. Sydney: n.p., 1996. Print.

8. An article in a journal

Author's name. "Title." *Publication details*. Medium of Publication.

An article in a journal has a different format from a book. The title of the article is placed in quotation marks while the journal title is in italics. The volume number, year of publication (in parenthesis), a colon, the inclusive page numbers, and a period follow the journal title.

Example 9: Kim, Praise. "Building Better Vocabulary." *Journal of Second Language Writing*, 20 (2011): 237-245. Print.

9. An article in a newspaper

Author's last name, first name. "Title." *Publication details*. Medium of Publication.

If the newspaper is locally published, write the city in square brackets, not underlined, after the newspaper name. Nationally or internationally published newspapers do not need to have the city included. Put the publication in italics and not the title.
If the newspaper is in sections (A, B, C) then include the section and pagination.

Example 9: Norland, Paul. "Afghan Bombing Campaign Kills Scores." *International Herald Tribune* 19 August 2011, A3. Print.

10. An article in a magazine

Like a newspaper, italicize the publication not the title. Include the complete date after the title of the magazine followed a colon (:) and pagination.

Example 10: Gibbs, Nancy. "Sex and Power: Why Powerful Men Abuse Women." *Time*. May 2011:67-71. Print.

11. An anonymous article

"Title." *Publication details*. Include the complete date after the title of the magazine followed a colon (:) and pagination. Medium of Publication.

Example 11: "The New America." *Economist*. 30 June 2011:101-106. Print.

12. Citing Electronic Publications

Author's name. "Title." *Title of the source*. Publication details. Medium of Publication. Date of access. URL (if required).

1. Medium of Publication. The uniform resource locater (URL) is no longer necessary as a URL can often change. Instead, the medium of publication for a web source is simply "Web".
2. Date: Two dates are required when citing online information. First, cite the date of the publication as it appears on the site. In addition, the date that it is accessed (when you view the information) is also required. Place the date after the medium of publication.

Example 12: Kim, Rahn. "Seoulites Go to the Polls." *Korean Times*. 20 July 2011. Web. 27 Oct. 2011.

13. An Online book

Author's name. "Title." Publication details. *Electronic publication details*. Date of access and URL.

14. An electronic article in a newspaper or magazine.

Follow the same procedures for a print source and add the date it is accessed and the URL.

Example 13: Lee, Robert. "Seoul Plans Women-only Subway Cars." *Korean Herald*. 20 July 2011. Web. 27 October 2011.

Tip

Citing sources in another language (non English)

In academic English writing, all non-English sources should be translated into English. When using information from a Korea sources, all details including author, title, and publishing details should be written in English.

Example 1: 김태훈. *사람의 힘*. 부산:만화 출판사, 2004

Example 2: Kim, Tae Hoon. *The Power of Love*. Busan: Manhwa Press, 2004

Source	Citation
Book by a single author	Author's last name, first name. *Title of the book*. Publication details. Medium of Publication.
Two or more books by the same author	1st book: Author's name. *Title of the book*. Publication details. Medium of Publication. 2nd book: ---. *Title of the book*. Publication details.
A book with more than one author	Authors name (Bracken, Daniel, Irene Parker, and Diana Tully). *Title of the book*. Publication details. Medium of Publication.
An article from a reference book	Author's name. "Title of section". *Title of the book*. Publication details. Medium of Publication.
A book with no author	*Title*. Publication details. (Italicize source name). Medium of Publication.
Government Publications	Author. Government that issued it. Agency or department. *Title*. Publication details. Medium of Publication.
A book without publication details	When publishing details (place, publisher, or date) are absent, provide abbreviations for missing information. n.p. No place of publication provided n.p. No publisher information provided n.d. No date provided n.pag. No pagination provided
An article in a journal	Author. "Title of the article." *Title of the journal*. Publication details. Medium of Publication. Publication details will include the journal title, the volume number, and the year of publication (in parenthesis), a colon, the inclusive page numbers, and a period. Medium of Publication.
An article in a newspaper	Author's name. "Title." *Title of the newspaper*. Publication details. If the newspaper is in sections (A, B, C) then include the section and pagination.
An article in a magazine	Author's name. "Title." *Title of the magazine*. Publication details. Include the complete date after the title of the magazine followed a colon (:) and pagination.
An anonymous article	"Title of the article." Publication details.
A document from an Internet site.	Author's name. "Title." Publication details. Medium of Publication. Date of access. URL (if required).

Activity 1

Use the following information to create a Works Cited page in your notebook.

Book 1
Author: Don Brown
Title: The Thinking Man's Guide to a Better Birth
Publisher: Harper Collins
Date: 2000
Pages: 109-110
City: New York

Book 2
Authors: Ray Grant, John Lee, Peter Negron
Title: Vampire Wars
Publisher: Hartman Murray
Date: 2007
Pages: 225-228
City: London

Book 3
Authors: Ray Grant, John Lee, Peter Negron
Title: Surviving a Zombie Invasion: A Practical Guide to Staying Alive
Publisher: Hartman Murray
Date: 2010
Page: 7

Book 4
Authors: Tim Hall, Sharon Park Colum Kienzle, Jeremy Castilleja
Title: Earthquake Engineering
Publisher: Random House
Date: 1996
Page: 114
City: Chicago

Print source
Title: Sparkling Daegu
Seoul 2009
Department of Tourism and Leisure Planning
Ministry of Culture, Sports, and Tourism
Page: 21-27

Journal
Authors: Justin Collins, William Lee
Journal of Applied Physics
Title: Energy Transfer in Nanowire Solar Cells
Volume 106 pages 211-245
2008

Magazine
Author: Ian White
Title: One Night in Manila
Time
2008 February edition.
Pages; 23-31

Internet Source
Title: The Wonderful Wonder Girls: Our Time is Now!
Website: Billboard
2010 March 20
http://www.billboard.com/#/new-releases

After learning about what plagiarism is and how to avoid it, fill out both contracts. Remove the bottom contract, and give it to your professor. Keep the top contract for yourself to remind you about your commitment to academic integrity.

Plagiarism Contract

I, ______________________________, hereby promise to uphold my credibility by avoiding plagiarism in my presentation materials. I will cite all the sources that I use from the Internet and from other places that are not from my ideas and creation. If I am caught plagiarizing or using materials from outside resources without proper citations, I will accept the consequences of receiving a zero on the project at hand.

Date: ______________________________ Class: ____________________

Printed Name: ______________________________

Student Number: ______________________________

Signature: ______________________________

____

....

Plagiarism Contract

I, ______________________________, hereby promise to uphold my credibility by avoiding plagiarism in my presentation materials. I will cite all the sources that I use from the Internet and from other places that are not from my ideas and creation. If I am caught plagiarizing or using materials from outside resources without proper citations, I will accept the consequences of receiving a zero on the project at hand.

Date: ______________________________ Class: ____________________

Printed Name: ______________________________

Student Number: ______________________________

Signature: ______________________________

____

Write On(Revised Edition)

A Guide for Practice and Progression in English Writing

Publisher | Chung, KyuSang
Printed by | Sungkyunkwan University Press
Publication date | February 21 2018

Writers | Cameron Bramall
Bridget McGregor
David Roberts
Project Coordinator | Yoon, Yousook

Sungkyunkwan University Press
25-2 Sungkyunkwan-ro, Jongno-gu
Seoul 03063, Korea
Tel: 82-2-760-1253~4, Fax: 82-2-762-7452
http://press.skku.edu

ISBN 979-11-5550-212-9 13740